What others are saying about
The Passion of Christ: A Gay Vision

"*The Passion of Christ: A Gay Vision* by Kittredge Cherry and Douglas Blanchard is transformative in the most profound sense of the word. Reimagining Jesus as a contemporary gay man, these images shock us with their deep familiarity and emotional dissidence, forcing us to rethink ingrained ideas about goodness, suffering, fear, loathing, and transcendence. Whether you are religious or not, it is impossible to read *The Passion of Christ* without having your basic beliefs shaken and expanded."

—Michael Bronski, professor of gender and sexuality at Harvard University
and author of *A Queer History of the United States*

"Author Kittredge Cherry and Douglas Blanchard, whose paintings grace this book, knock it out of the ball park. I was deeply moved by this retelling of the Easter story."

—Rev. Troy Perry, founder of Metropolitan Community Churches

"What an amazing read. Together Douglas Blanchard's paintings and Kittredge Cherry's text forced me to see Jesus again, not frozen in time by a Renaissance sculptor or idolized in gold on a Byzantine icon, but as a living, breathing, sensual son of man whom I want to know more intimately not just as 'Savior and Lord' but as a close friend and confidant."

—Rev. Dr. Mel White, founder of Soulforce and author of
Stranger at the Gate: To be Gay and Christian in America

"I have come to expect to be moved, challenged, and enlightened by the work of Kittredge Cherry and this latest offering has not disappointed. The combination of the contemporary images along with pertinent theological insight is deeply effective and brings to life the Passion not only for the LGBT community but for all people struggling to find themselves in the narrative and make sense of their faith."

—Rev. Sharon Ferguson, M.A., chief executive of the Lesbian
and Gay Christian Movement (United Kingdom)

"*The Passion of Christ* is a beautiful work of contextual theology. Cherry and Blanchard respond powerfully to Jesus' question of 'Who do you say that I am?' from a contemporary queer perspective. This marvelous book will speak not only to LGBTIQ Christians, but also to anyone who is passionate about creating a more just world for the marginalized and excluded."

—Rev. Patrick S. Cheng, Ph.D., theology professor at Episcopal Divinity School
and author of *From Sin to Amazing Grace: Discovering the Queer Christ*

"The ancient story of Jesus acquires new layers of meaning when read through queer eyes. Suffering is more pronounced when depicted in real time. The divine leaps from these pages into open hearts. Few will view this art and read these commentaries without weeping for injustice and committing to love."

—Mary Hunt, Ph.D., co-director, Women's Alliance for Theology, Ethics and Ritual

"What a joy it is to hold, read, and contemplate a book such as this! For centuries, the Passion of Jesus Christ has been a favorite topic for artists. Douglas Blanchard's inspired and powerful contemporary reworking of this theme, with its brilliant and touching echoes of so much that is sadly true in our world, shares in this long heritage. Kittredge Cherry's prayerful commentary on the twenty-four panels helps move us to a place of profound theological reflection. Not only is this a compellingly gay and much-needed re-visioning of the central Christian mystery. It also defiantly reaffirms our common humanity."

—Donald L. Boisvert, Ph.D., religion professor at Concordia University, priest in the Anglican Church of Canada, and author of *Sanctity and Male Desire: A Gay Reading of Saints*

"The great theologian and physician Albert Schweitzer once famously noted that each new epoch has sought and found a new Jesus. This is 'the only way in which it could make Him live.' Here Kittredge Cherry and Douglas Blanchard make Jesus live. For new trials and times, new faces and places, challenging our conceptions, preconceptions, and misconceptions."

—S. Brent Plate, Ph.D., religion professor at Hamilton College and author of *Blasphemy: Art that Offends*

"*The Passion of Christ: A Gay Vision* gives new meaning to Christ's Passion, and also new feeling—feelings that connect the story of Christ's mission, suffering, and new life to our own, not just as LGBT people, but for all thought 'queer' by 'the powers that be.' Not only did it stretch my spirit, but I also learned much about Christian art, scripture, theology, and history that challenges prevalent church assumptions. This is a great contribution to art about Jesus. Paintings, interpretations, and afterword are all quite profound."

—Rev. Chris Glaser, author of *Coming Out as Sacrament* and weekly blogger of Progressive Christian Reflections (chrisglaser.blogspot.com)

"Peopled with figures recognizable from today's cityscapes, including protestors, lawmakers, and the nameless abjected, Blanchard's vivid images highlight the beauty and pain of contemporary LGBT experience. In this world, resurrection is communal, and divine and human loves transgress boundaries. Cherry's rich, resonant commentary provides fertile resources for reflection, meditation, study, and prayer."

—Susannah Cornwall, Ph.D., advanced research fellow in theology and religion at the University of Exeter, UK, and author of *Controversies in Queer Theology*

"*The Passion of Christ* is a wonderful book that should have great appeal not only to the LGBTQ community but to all for whom the Passion of Christ is spiritually significant. The introductions by Kittredge Cherry and Douglas Blanchard provide invaluable background to the history of depictions of the passion. The paintings are provocative and powerful; the reflections that accompany them are sensitive interweavings of scripture and contemporary experience. As a Christian theologian I am deeply grateful for this fine work."

—Theodore W. Jennings, Ph.D., Bible professor at Chicago Theological Seminary and author of *The Man Jesus Loved: Homoerotic Narratives from the New Testament*

the passion of christ

a gay vision

BY KITTREDGE CHERRY

ART BY DOUGLAS BLANCHARD

AFTERWORD BY TOBY JOHNSON

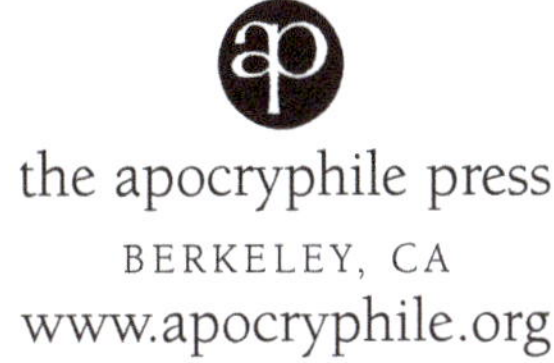

the apocryphile press
BERKELEY, CA
www.apocryphile.org

apocryphile press
BERKELEY, CA

Apocryphile Press
1700 Shattuck Ave #81
Berkeley, CA 94709
www.apocryphile.org

Text copyright © 2014 by Kittredge Cherry
Art copyright © 2014 by Douglas Blanchard
All rights reserved.

ISBN 9781955821490

Photo of Kittredge Cherry by Audrey Lockwood
Photo of Douglas Blanchard by Cristina Vergano

Unless otherwise noted, scripture quotations are from the Revised Standard Version of the Bible, copyright © 1946, 1952, and 1971 National Council of the Churches of Christ in the United States of America. Used by permission. All rights reserved.

*Scripture quotations marked with an asterisk are from the Inclusive Language Lectionary, copyright © 1985-88 National Council of the Churches of Christ in the USA, based on the Revised Standard Version of the Bible, copyright © 1946, 1952, and 1971 National Council of the Churches of Christ in the USA. Used by permission. All rights reserved.

Great art is not a matter of presenting one side or another,
but presenting a picture so full of the contradictions, tragedies,
[and] insights of the period that the impact
is at once disturbing and satisfying.

—PAULI MURRAY

OTHER BOOKS BY KITTREDGE CHERRY

Art That Dares
Gay Jesus, Woman Christ, and More

Jesus in Love
A Novel

Jesus in Love: At the Cross
A Novel

Hide and Speak
A Coming Out Guide

Womansword
What Japanese Words Say About Women

Equal Rites
Lesbian and Gay Worship, Ceremonies, and Celebrations
(with Zalmon O. Sherwood)

Contents

Author's Introduction

BY KITTREDGE CHERRY

Jesus challenges viewers by arriving as a young gay man of today in the Passion of Christ paintings by Douglas Blanchard. The artist takes the most important narrative in Western culture and rescues it from fundamentalists and also from over-familiarity. Blanchard, a self-proclaimed "very agnostic believer," breaks the lethal illusion that Jesus belongs exclusively to a particular time or group. He used the series to grapple with his own faith struggles as a gay New Yorker who witnessed the 9/11 terrorist attacks. The artist revitalizes an old story by telling it with new images featuring modern dress, an urban setting, and a diverse cast of contemporary characters. The purpose of reflecting on the Passion is not necessarily to worship Christ, but to remember the ongoing cycle of human violence, and to seek a way to move from suffering to freedom. The Passion story invites each viewer to stand at the cross as a compassionate witness—and to take up their own cross, whatever it may be.

A gay Passion is crucial now even for non-believers because Christianity is being used to justify hate and discrimination against lesbian, gay, bisexual, and transgender (LGBT) people. Queer people have been labeled "sinners," denied civil rights and economic access, erased from history, and have sometimes been beaten or killed in the name of Jesus. Yet Blanchard chooses to reclaim the Passion story instead of rejecting it. "I'm not prepared to concede the Gospel to people who believe that they own the copyright to it, and who use it as a cudgel to dominate others," he says. The gay vision salvages Jesus from the wreckage of the culture wars, disrupting all attempts to find easy answers. The artist's gay consciousness transforms the dangerous mythologies that arose around Jesus.

Using a realistic figurative style, Blanchard paints a shockingly new vision with exceptional artistic skill and symbolic depth. His Jesus stands up to priests, bankers, politicians, soldiers, and police—all of whom look eerily similar to the people holding those jobs today. In Blanchard's gay vision, Jesus is jeered by fundamentalists, tortured by Marine look-alikes, and rises again to enjoy homoerotic moments with God. The 24 paintings in the gay Passion series portray Jesus in a modern city as he experiences his final days, including the arrest, trial, crucifixion, and resurrection. The hero of his series doesn't appear obviously gay, nor does he look like the stereotypical Jesus. The artist lets Jesus' actions speak for themselves and leaves room for the viewer to inhabit the image. Jesus is not the only gay person in this vision of the Passion. He attracts surprisingly diverse crowds in which some of his best friends—and perhaps a few of his enemies—appear to be queer. By placing the Passion story in an up-to-date cityscape, the artist raises revealing questions: If Jesus came back today, would he be crucified all over again? Would we even recognize him?

The word "passion" entered the English language from the Latin term *passio,* which means suffering, and can refer specifically to the suffering of Christ in his final days. Later it came to mean any strong emotion or desire. In Blanchard's vision God identifies with the oppressed, including queer people, so passionately that gay experience becomes God's own experience through Jesus. This extraordinary Christ figure fights for justice and yet he cannot be pigeonholed. He doesn't play favorites. He goes beyond liberation theology's God of the oppressed. Jesus is incarnated anew as one of today's queer people, but he doesn't stay in the gay ghetto. He is a healthy young white man, but he befriends women, people of color, the disabled, the elderly, and the poor, as well as queers. Blanchard's vision is prophetic because he painted a world that is coming into being: a society where LGBT people mix easily with everyone else. Not only Jesus, but also the people around him are visibly transformed by his death-defying journey from prison to paradise. The importance of the subject, the talent of the artist, and the maturity of his understanding combine to create powerful masterpieces for our time.

Blanchard bears witness to the truth of human cruelty without glorifying violence, submission, or sacrifice. His paintings make explicit the connection between Christ's crucifixion and all acts of aggression, particularly today's anti-gay violence in the name of religion. Like so many other prophets and liberators, Jesus was killed by the forces that oppose love, justice, equality, and freedom. LGBT people often identify with the hurt and humiliation that Jesus experienced on the cross. Too many LGBT lives have been a torturous journey to Calvary in which mistreatment by the church crushed the faith out of them. Jesus himself said, "Whatever you did to the least of these, you did to me." In that sense, it is entirely appropriate to see Christ in the faces of those who are scapegoated and attacked for being queer. Many LGBT people and allies have rejected Christianity, especially the Passion, because of its connection to domination and violence. Theologies of atonement have used the Passion to sanction war and personal violence. In Blanchard's vision, the Passion becomes a way to question, dismantle, and free people from deadly religious ideologies.

The series remains true to the Jesus of scripture and traditional Christian faith, with one big exception: the addition of a gay orientation for Jesus. Nobody knows whether the historical Jesus was homosexual, although some scholars do think so. The gospel of John describes Jesus interacting with his special "beloved" disciple, usually considered to be John himself. Nowhere does the Bible mention that Jesus had a wife. Jesus didn't discuss homosexuality directly, but he did upset religious authorities by breaking gender rules, befriending sexual outcasts, and teaching love without limits. Whether he was gay or straight, Jesus remains celibate in the eyes of many Christians. That belief is not necessarily contradicted by Blanchard's art. In this series, Jesus appears to consummate his homoerotic desires only after his physical death and only with God.

Blanchard restores LGBT people to a place in the Passion, ending the long conspiracy of silence.

Blanchard restores LGBT people to a place in the Passion, ending the long conspiracy of silence about their contributions to Christianity. The queer quest for God became invisible, even though LGBT people helped build the church from the beginning. The queer aspect opens up a new entry point to the Passion story, especially for those who feel excluded from the church. Jesus takes on a gay orientation in order to affirm that LGBT lives today are sacred. The result is revelatory. Viewers are pushed to increase the places they look for the risen Christ. The queer lens encourages fresh understanding of the cross, and what it means to be part of the body of Christ.

The artist expected the series to be a "career killer," alienating both the secular art world and conservative Christians, but he dared to paint it anyway. The paintings helped him wrestle with the role of religion in the terrorist attacks of September 11, 2001. His studio is located on the Lower East Side of Manhattan, about two miles from the World Trade Center site. He began painting the life of Christ a few months before the terrorist attack there plunged him into a crisis of faith that is reflected in his Passion. It took him four years to complete the series.

The risky project turned into his biggest success. Like the black Jesus and woman Christ before him, the gay Jesus enlightens all by filling the void left when a disadvantaged group is excluded from sacred stories. The world needs a gay Christ figure at the start of the 21st century. The images speak both to the faithful and to nonbelievers, serving a dual purpose as art objects and devotional tools. People from many different backgrounds marveled that Blanchard's

Passion is "accessible but profound" and "disturbing, but ultimately glorious." Some were moved to tears. Viewers embraced the Passion at galleries, in print magazines, and across the Internet. Everyone seems to have a different favorite out of the 24 images, and individuals are drawn to different paintings at various points in their lives.

The art also angered conservatives. Just as Jesus himself faced opposition, the gay Passion series was attacked by right-wing fundamentalists. They condemned the whole concept as a "perverted" and "blasphemous" effort to promote "the homosexual agenda." In the culture wars the cross has been reduced from its historical complexity to a litmus test for salvation or eternal damnation. Blanchard was not willing to concede the gospel to those who felt entitled to use it as a weapon for dominating others. His work challenges fundamentalism not with the usual counter-polemic, but by presenting a more nuanced alternative. Far from being blasphemous, painting the gay Passion was an act of moral courage in a critically engaged form of Christianity.

It may be painful to witness the violent death of Jesus, but his story resounds in the human spirit. The Passion narrative is deeply ingrained in Western culture. For Christians his sacrifice redeems a broken world. Jesus embodies the archetype of the hero who leaves the ordinary world, triumphs over difficult challenges, and returns as a savior with power to benefit others. Not just any hero, Jesus also fits the mythic patterns of the martyr who dies for the sake of others and the god-man who dies and is reborn. The fact that Jesus personifies common archetypes does not diminish his power or validity. The divine drama becomes a model for psychological growth, or what theologians call redemption and sanctification. And yet Jesus is also the anti-hero, an everyman figure who is irrevocably, irredeemably human. The way to overcome death is not by denial but by moving through it to rebirth. For believers, the Passion is the ultimate affirmation that God chooses to stand in solidarity with humankind.

Portraying a queer Christ presents unique artistic challenges. It's difficult to visually code Jesus as gay without sexualizing him or reducing him to a stereotype. For some viewers the slightest hint can indicate that Jesus is gay, and anything more seems too sexually explicit or "like a billboard." On the other hand, the image of Jesus is so closely associated with right-wing homophobes that some viewers must see an out-and-proud Jesus before they can believe he is gay. Blanchard solves the dilemma by keeping Jesus' sexual orientation invisible, except in a couple of post-resurrection panels. Some progressive Bible scholars do argue that the historical Jesus had a homosexual relationship, but Blanchard gracefully sidesteps that issue. Before the resurrection his Jesus is actually less homoerotic than many church-approved masterpieces by Michelangelo and other great artists of the past. People call the series a "gay Passion" for short, but Blanchard's title makes it clear that he painted an unconditional "The Passion of Christ." The word Christ is both a religious title and a blessed state to which anyone can aspire. Only the subtitle specifies that it is "a gay vision."

Images of a queer Christ are on the rise now in Western culture. Religious excuses for discrimination against LGBT people have made the emergence of the gay Jesus necessary and inevitable. When other artists have addressed queer Christian themes, they often depict a

Christ figure alone, in a same-sex couple, or within a segregated LGBT community. Some insert a standard-issue Christ figure into the current LGBT scene. The result can come across as inflammatory or a cheap shot. Sometimes Jesus appears to be nothing more than the gratuitously sexy object of homoerotic fantasy. Blanchard avoids all those traps. He doesn't combine gay and Christian symbols to be sensational. In fact, he downplays both the gay *and* the Christian elements. His genius is showing LGBT people, including a gay Jesus, integrated in contemporary life—and in the afterlife. Queer Christian art arose during the modern era, with its suspicion of miracles and happy endings. Few artists cared to portray a queer vision of the resurrection. Blanchard, painting from a place of faith, lavishes attention on Jesus' exploits after he rises from the dead. For him the Passion is not an artistic device or visual shorthand, but a living, breathing mystery. He is able to mine its depths for the riches still buried there. His deep synthesis of both gay and Christian experience results in images that are ideal for intellectual and spiritual reflection.

Blanchard finds ways to communicate without cliché about Jesus' sexuality and about another thorny issue: his spirituality. Contemporary artists find it hard to depict Jesus without becoming sanctimonious or trite. In Christian tradition Jesus is fully divine and fully human, or "very God and very man." At first glance most of Blanchard's Passion paintings appear to show a totally human Jesus. A closer look reveals hints of holiness—but with a postmodern sensibility. Most of the paintings have no overt symbols to show that the protagonist is Jesus, other than his name inextricably painted onto the faux frames. Cues to his sacred identity tend to be everyday hints of holiness that viewers might recognize in their own lives if they paused to look. Blanchard discards the predictable image of Jesus with beard and white robe. Some say his Jesus looks like rock star David Bowie. He is modeled after contemporary men and the earliest images of Christ, which date back to the third century. They showed Jesus as a beardless youth, handsome and athletic. Blanchard's Jesus almost always looks impassive and at peace, no matter what is happening. Some perceive him as confused. He is usually at the center of every composition. In many cases he looks directly forward, gazing back into the eyes of the viewer like a Byzantine icon.

Throughout history, and even now, most art about the Passion was commissioned by churches. Blanchard was confirmed in the Episcopal Church in 1982 and remains an active if agnostic Episcopalian, but he did not paint the Passion for a church. He created it as his own individual artistic statement. Christianity is not just a source of visual code for him, but the code by which he lives.

Born and raised in Dallas, Texas, Blanchard earned a BFA in painting from the Kansas City Art Institute in 1981, an MA in art history from Washington University in St. Louis in 1986, and an MFA cum laude from the New York Academy of Art in 1993. He has taught art and art history at Bronx Community College of the City University of New York since 2001. His art explores gay experience, such as the Stonewall uprising, as well as classical mythology, history, and current events. He lived through the AIDS crisis and it serves as an inconspicuous backdrop to his Passion series. One of his favorite subjects is AIDS activist/artist David Wojnarowicz. Before starting the

Passion of Christ, Blanchard painted Wojnarowicz as an AIDS martyr traveling a kind of gritty Stations of the Cross in a series titled *Shadows*. After he finished Christ's Passion, Blanchard began a second, more extensive Wojnarowicz series, which was still in progress in 2014. For the future he dreams of painting Jesus again in ways that will further expand how people see him. "If I do another version of the Passion, then I would make Christ racially mixed, or racially indeterminate," he said.

Blanchard, who is an art history professor as well as an artist, draws deeply from the rich artistic heritage of Christian art. The structure of his Passion is art historical as much as Biblical or liturgical. In general he breaks the story into standard scenes that have been painted by the great artists of history, even though they do not all appear in scripture. Blanchard deliberately updated the language for the titles, just as he did for the imagery. Thus, "The Ascension" becomes "Jesus Returns to God" and so on.

Viewers enter effortlessly into Blanchard's Passion series, but enjoyment can be intensified by decoding the symbolism and layers of meaning. The more you look, the more you see. For example, his intricate visual vocabulary includes background arches that form down-to-earth halos around the head of Jesus. Watch closely for recurring characters—and check out the frames. Blanchard uses a trompe l'oeil technique to trick viewers into believing that the paintings are mounted into separate frames. Actually he painted the frames, numbers, and titles directly onto each wooden panel so that they could never be taken out of context. The optical illusion is enhanced when elements from inside the image spill over onto the frame.

The earliest prototypes for the gay Passion are located in the Catacombs of Rome.

The earliest prototypes for the gay Passion series are located in the Catacombs of Rome. These underground burial places contain sculptures and frescoes from as long ago as the second century. The scenes in Blanchard's Passion that date back to the Catacombs are Jesus' entry to Jerusalem, the Last Supper, and Jesus carrying his cross—but not the crucifixion. Many people are surprised to learn that Jesus dying on the cross—the scene that dominates Christian art—was not depicted until a thousand years after he died. Christian symbols were disguised out of necessity during the early period of persecution. Before the fourth century Christians were killed for their refusal to worship Roman gods. Thus the cross was camouflaged as an anchor, a Roman symbol of hope. Written accounts of the Passion gave meaning to the martyrdoms, and these texts gained prominence over the more peaceful gnostic versions of the gospel. Still the Passion remained absent from art even after Christianity gained official recognition in 313. Jesus was usually presented as the Good Shepherd, a miracle worker, or the king of an earthly paradise until the ninth century. Perhaps it is no coincidence that the church was also relatively tolerant of homosexuality during its first millennium. A few artists began to portray Jesus on the cross in the fourth century, but he was vibrant and victorious, head held high. The crucifixion and the resurrection were presented together as one unified victory.

The rise of Passion imagery in art was accompanied by the execution of heretics, witches, and "sodomites."

Scholars have concocted various theories to explain why early Christian artists avoided the crucifixion. The traditional view is that they were too ashamed and horrified by the way Jesus died, or perhaps just not as "advanced" as later Christians. Progressive theologians offer a happier explanation: For the first thousand years of church history, believers had a life-centered spirituality. Their artwork suggests that they cared more about how Christ lived than how he died. The church was also relatively accepting of homosexuality in this period. With the Passion viewers mourn not only the death of Jesus, but the passing of an earlier form of Christianity when his crucifixion was not the central model to be re-enacted in churches, on battlefields, and in the human soul.

The Passion cycle as it is known today, and as Blanchard envisions it, was developed by artists in Christianity's second millennium. The era was marked by the entanglement of the church, political power, and military force, often with brutal results. The groundwork was laid in the year 800 with the crowning of Charlemagne as the first emperor of the Holy Roman Empire. His armies united most of western Europe with bloody military campaigns, imposing Roman Catholicism on the people that they conquered. The earliest image of the dead Jesus on the cross was sculpted around 970 by the descendants of Saxons crushed by Charlemagne. Known as the Gero Crucifix, it ushered in a progression of increasingly realistic crucifixion art that continues into the present. The rise of Passion imagery in art was accompanied by the conquest of "heathens" abroad, and the execution of heretics, witches, and "sodomites" at home.

The death penalty for homosexuality was first put into church law in 1120 by the Council of Nablus. Brutalization of queers became one shard from a wholeness that had been shattered. (An excellent book on the subject is *Saving Paradise: How Christianity Traded Love of This World for Crucifixion and Empire* by Rita Nakashima Brock and Rebecca Ann Parker.)

Scenes of Christ suffering in the Passion cycle were painted by virtually every great European artist in the Medieval, Renaissance, and Baroque periods, from Giotto to Michelangelo, Da Vinci, Caravaggio, Rubens, and Rembrandt. Every episode was painted thousands of times, but the crucifixion was the most common. Each scene spawned its own iconography. The imagery became more gruesome as artists continued to place greater emphasis on the humanity of Jesus. Blanchard acknowledges that he was especially inspired by *The Small Passion,* a series of 36 woodcuts from 1511 by German Renaissance artist Albrecht Dürer. Like Dürer, Blanchard devotes about a quarter of his series to events after the resurrection.

The concept of Blanchard's Passion was also influenced by the Stations of the Cross, a set of artistic images used for meditation on Christ's suffering and death. The Stations of the Cross remains one of the most popular devotions among Catholics and some Protestants, especially during Holy Week and on Good Friday. Walking through the Stations helps people get in touch with their deep feelings, their passion, as they stop to pray and reflect at each scene. Also known as the Via Crucis (Way of the Cross) or Via Dolorosa (Way of Sorrows), the images line the walls of almost every Roman Catholic church as a series of relief plaques or paintings. The Stations arose through popular piety among Christian pilgrims who visited Jerusalem as far back as the fourth century. They retraced Jesus' footsteps through Jerusalem, stopping along the way to recall his final days. These Stations of the Cross were imported to Europe by the Franciscans in the 1400s to recreate the Jerusalem experience for a broader audience. At first there were many variations, but the current set of fourteen Stations was standardized in 1731. The traditional fourteen Stations begin when Jesus is condemned to death and stop with his burial. Contrary to early Christian art, there was no resurrection. Starting in the 1960s it became popular to add a fifteenth Station with Jesus rising on Easter.

The importance of Christian art began to fade in the eighteenth century, but occasionally secular artists still produced well-known works on Christian subjects. With the rise of secular society, people started to collect earlier Christian masterpieces as art objects instead of using them for worship. Christian artists became marginalized, but at least two famous twentieth-century artists aspired to treat the whole Passion narrative: French expressionists Henri Matisse and Georges Rouault. Like Blanchard, Rouault put Jesus in some contemporary settings. Smokestacks loom in the background of a scene from his Passion series, painted in the 1930s. Matisse combined all fourteen Stations of the Cross into one starkly modern mural when he designed the Chapel of the Rosary in Vence, France. Matisse considered the chapel to be his masterpiece, but visitors were shocked by his Way of the Cross when the chapel opened in 1951. Other twentieth-century masters known for painting the crucifixion include Italian surrealist Salvador Dali and Russian painter Marc Chagall.

Blanchard's work is not so much influenced by modern religious art as it is parallel to it. Like Matisse, Rouault, and the rest, he draws on the past to update the Passion for a new era with his own unique voice and style. The resources that he draws on from twentieth-century art seem more political than religious. He invents a new kind of social realism, finding inspiration for his Passion in anti-war art, such as the paintings of soldiers abusing prisoners by figurative expressionist Leon Golub. His aesthetic is also rooted in photography that documents lynchings, the civil rights movement, and the Holocaust. He gained ideas for composition and dramatic lighting from films, especially Orson Welles movies. Blanchard's modern influences are literary as well as visual. His views about the Passion were shaped by writers William Blake, W.H. Auden, Paul Tillich, and Hannah Arendt, whose work led him to the Christological allegory of Herman Melville's novella *Billy Budd*.

By painting the Passion Blanchard became part of a resurgence of figurative and religious art in the late 20th and early 21st centuries. A growing number of individual artists like Blanchard are letting their faith show in their work. New religious art continues to be commissioned by churches and cathedrals. In today's "post-Christian" culture, faith-based art coexists with art that uses Christian iconography to make secular statements or even for deliberate shock value. Huge controversies have erupted as conservatives tried to censor Christian imagery in museum-sponsored contemporary art, such as *Piss Christ* by Andres Serrano and the elephant-dung encrusted *Holy Virgin Mary* by Chris Ofili.

Queer Christian art generally uses two complementary approaches: Artists either take a defiant stand that attacks Christianity as an instrument of oppression, or else they reclaim Christian imagery to support LGBT spiritualities. Both methods cause controversy. One of the latest battles to gain national attention was sparked by David Wojnarowicz, the gay artist/activist who has been painted many times by Blanchard. The Wojnarowicz video *A Fire in My Belly* was censored by the Smithsonian Institution in 2010 when Christian conservatives objected. They denounced the video as anti-Christian "hate speech" because it showed ants crawling over Jesus on a crucifix to symbolize gay suffering due to AIDS. Wojnarowicz made the video back in 1987 at a time when thousands of gay Americans were dying of AIDS every year. In the late 1980s grief over the AIDS crisis led artists to the most daring queer Christian theme of all: the gay Jesus. The Passion became the predominant subject in queer Christian art. LGBT people are still scapegoated, so an ongoing empathy with the sufferings of Christ continues to manifest in art. Other artists from around the world who have portrayed a gay Jesus include Bill Burch, Alex Donis, Becki Jayne Harrelson, Alfred Hrdlicka, Carlos Latuff, William Hart McNichols, Dirk Vanden, and Andrew Craig Williams.

Blanchard's Passion is emerging as one of the most respected artworks to blend Christian and LGBT themes. Only a few other artists have tackled the ambitious project of re-imagining Christ's whole Passion from a queer perspective. The best-known example is Swedish photographer Elisabeth Ohlson Wallin. Her 1998 *Ecce Homo* series became one of Europe's most notorious art exhibits. She used contemporary LGBT models to recreate famous masterpieces from the life of Christ. Subsequently other photographers did gay versions, including Fernando Bayona Gonzalez of Spain and Robert Recker of Germany. Starting in the mid-1990s, New Mexico artist Delmas Howe spent about a decade painting the eighteen large canvases of *Stations: A Gay Passion.* The series is loosely based on the Stations of the Cross. Set in the gay sex piers of New York City, Howe's series mixes nudity and sadomasochistic motifs with references to classic religious art. It commemorates gay men who died of AIDS because they celebrated their sexuality, a kind of gay Passion. In 2013 Tennessee artist Mary Button painted *Stations of the Cross: The Struggle for LGBT Equality.* Using bold colors and collage, Button shows that Jesus suffers with LGBT people. She juxtaposes his journey to Golgotha with milestones from the last 100 years of LGBT history, including Nazi persecution, the Lavender Scare, the Stonewall Rebellion, the assassination of gay politician Harvey Milk, the AIDS pandemic, the murder of transgender woman Rita Hester, and LGBT teen suicides.

Blanchard's gay Way of the Cross takes more subtle form than most. Maybe that explains why his Passion didn't make a big splash when it was first exhibited. The series tackles an enormous subject, but each individual oil painting is a modest 18-by-14 inch wooden panel. When hung together in a gallery, they do not evoke awe, but lure the viewer to look more closely and enter into the story. Their size creates intimacy and also enables them to adapt well to presentation in book format. The Passion premiered at the Leslie-Lohman Museum of Gay and Lesbian Art in New York City in spring 2004. The museum billed it as part of their *Undiscovered Gay Masters* series, but it may have been overshadowed by the male nudes and large canvases in other parts of the gallery. Blanchard had only completed the first twenty paintings, so the other panels were displayed in an unfinished state.

I decided to write about Blanchard's Passion because it touched me so deeply from the moment I first discovered it in 2005. That year I began sharing it on my LGBT spirituality website JesusInLove.org. I included five panels in my book *Art That Dares: Gay Jesus, Woman Christ, and More.* The book was launched in May 2007 with an exhibit at JHS Gallery in Taos, New Mexico. The com-

I decided to write about Blanchard's Passion because it touched me so deeply.

pleted Passion series was displayed together there for the first and only time in a group exhibit titled *Who Do You Say That I Am? Visions of Christ, Gender, and Justice.* Blanchard's series became the show's superstar, with almost half of the 24 panels in his series getting snapped up by collectors. Now they are scattered all across the country. My appreciation for the series deepened when I began posting commentaries on each individual painting during Holy Week 2011. Synergy sprang forth between word, image, and audience. I witnessed the power of the Passion to move people. The ideas expressed in this book were fertilized from the grassroots in the free-for-all debate of the blogosphere.

Doug and I have complementary skills and experiences, representing male and female, East Coast and West Coast. Our partnership on this book makes sense because we balance each other in some ways while leading parallel lives. Both of us were born in 1957 and raised in Middle America (Texas for him; Iowa for me). We both earned degrees in art history before moving to opposite coasts. Each of us had a conversion experience in the early 1980s that inspired us to switch to the denominations that we still call home. Raised in a Methodist mega-church in Dallas, Doug was confirmed as an Episcopalian in 1982. I grew up mostly secular with sporadic Presbyterian attendance, but was baptized in an interdenominational church in 1984. Soon I joined the LGBT-affirming Metropolitan Community Churches. In 1991 we both moved to the big cities in which we still live: He moved to New York and I went to Los Angeles. Without knowing about each other, we each spent the period from 2001 to 2005 working independently on projects presenting a gay-positive vision of the life of Christ. While he was painting the Passion series, I was writing my *Jesus in Love* novels. Guided by love for God and art, both Doug and I now find ourselves on the cutting-edge of the queer Christ trend.

The reputation of Blanchard's gay Passion has continued to grow over the years. The importance of the subject, the talent of the artist, and the maturity of his understanding combine to create powerful masterpieces for our time. Countless people have joined his Jesus on the queer pathway from prison to paradise, from bondage to freedom. The starting and ending points are a surprise, giving the series a scope well beyond the same old Stations of the Cross.

The scenes extend far into both the past and future, centuries before and after the lifespan of the historical Jesus. The distant past and the present converge in the image that begins the series. The magnificent final picture shows how Jesus has been transformed by timeless love that is stronger than death when the journey comes full circle. Updating the Passion for our age has revealed an ageless story of human suffering and the power of love to overcome it. ●

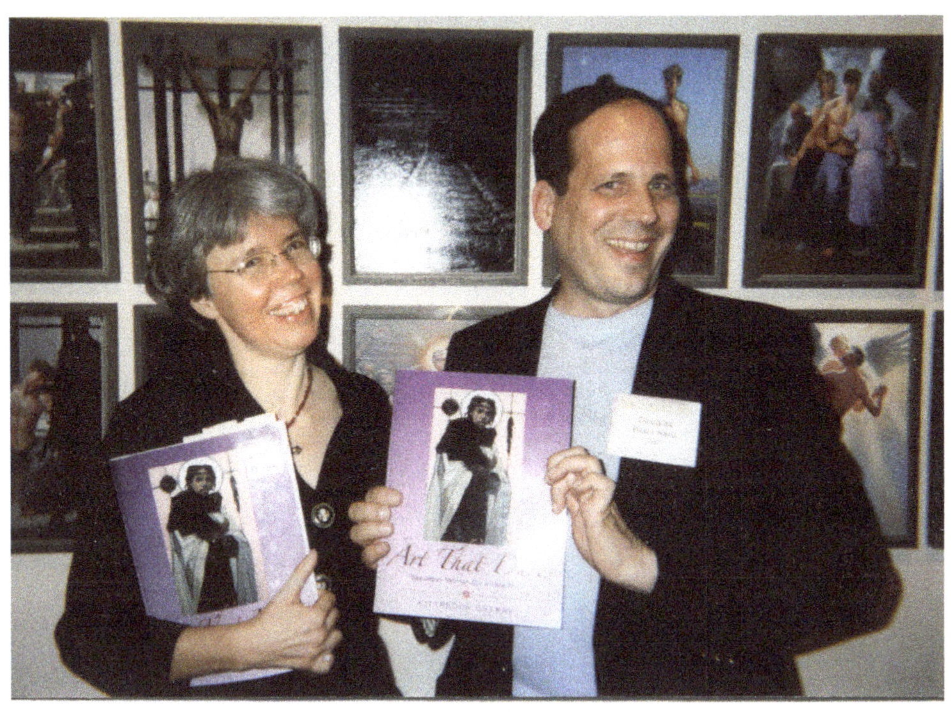

Kittredge Cherry and Douglas Blanchard met when all the paintings in "The Passion of Christ: A Gay Vision" were displayed together at JHS Gallery in Taos, New Mexico in May 2007.

PHOTO BY AUDREY LOCKWOOD.

Artist's Introduction

BY DOUGLAS BLANCHARD

The 24 panel series of *The Passion of Christ* is the only major religious work that I've ever done. And yet, I spent years preparing for it one way or another. It draws together themes that I've dealt with in other works most of my life. It is the most important painting project that I have done to date, and yet, I was definitely not confident about the outcome or the reception of the work when I embarked on it. I felt certain that it would be a career killer. Composers can make religious works and still be taken seriously, but artists can't. I'm not sure why, but it seems like religious content can only appear ironically in art, either as satire or as some kind of elegy over the loss of belief. I was certain that after a lot of work, this project would be panned, or much worse, simply ignored. My intentions in this work are neither ironic nor elegiac. I am quite serious about the story and its presentation. This is a story that still speaks directly to me (as well as many others) about all kinds of issues: justice and injustice, truth and authority, power and powerlessness, success and failure, mortality and immortality, flesh and spirit, life and death, and what all those things mean together.

I've always painted figuratively. I focus on the human image, human experience, and the human point of view. While I love and admire the great achievements of modern abstract art, I do not see the world in terms of abstraction or reductivism. I'm more interested in the world in all of its fullness, and in that human perspective which is all we have to find our way through it. I think of myself as being a kind of history painter, not in the sense of wanting to record or reconstruct history so much as to show meaning revealed (or perhaps created) in human drama. I'm less interested in the literal history of the events of Christ's death than I am in the Passion as a story that people live by.

I was initially inspired by a series of 36 small woodcuts by Albrecht Dürer known as *The Small Passion*. I considered doing something like a 14-panel Stations of the Cross, but decided that I was much more interested in the story and in the totality of its meaning than in any liturgical considerations. I returned to the earlier, much more free-form Passion series that prevailed before liturgies of the Stations were formalized in the 18th century. Dürer's Small Passion begins with the story of Adam and Eve, through the infancy of Christ, the events of His Passion and Death, the Resurrection, and finally the Last Judgment. I decided to concentrate on the events of the Passion and the Resurrection. Dürer began his series with a kind of introduction, an image of The Man of Sorrows. I decided to do something similar, and to present Him with the mysterious title 'Son of Man' from the Gospels. I portray Him with two prophets deeply concerned with suffering and redemption, Job and Isaiah. I added a coda to my series, a painting of the Trinity. These two paintings state at the beginning and at the end the whole theme of the series, which is God in solidarity with us.

I decided not to present anything like a literal retelling of the story in the Gospels, or some very literal-minded archaeological reconstruction of Roman Judea in the first century. I'm not interested in the historical Jesus of Nazareth, an alien figure to us from a very distant time, from a world that no longer exists, and speaking a language that is now almost extinct. I took my cue from Renaissance paintings. We always excuse their habit of setting biblical stories in 15th-century Flemish towns or the Tuscan countryside as a naïve ignorance of archaeology. There was nothing naïve about this. What mattered to people then was not the literal history, but the meaning of those stories for the here and now. Artists in their works told people to expect to find the Nativity in a Tuscan barn, to find the Virgin Mary with the saints in a Flemish flower garden, or to meet the suffering Christ in the streets of Siena. The artists didn't mean that quite literally, but they did intend for us to see these stories and their meanings played out again and again in the dramas that take place in front of us daily. I tried to do something similar in my paintings by setting the Passion in something like the modern world familiar to us. The cityscapes in my Passion series are nowhere in particular. They are based loosely on places I see regularly in New York.

There are no reliable descriptions or depictions of the historical Jesus of Nazareth. The traditional image that we have is a creation of later history. The earliest surviving depictions in art of Christ are from the third century, and are beardless youthful figures derived from images of the god Apollo. The doe-eyed, bearded, long-haired figure in a robe that we know does not appear fully formed until the sixth century. In some ways, I returned to that first tradition. I shed some of the gravitas of the conventional image by making Christ beardless and a little younger. Instead of remoteness and unapproachable sanctity, I decided for accessibility and charisma. I wanted Christ to be attractive in the fullest sense, sexually and spiritually, someone who draws people to Him. At the same time, I tried to avoid anything that smacked of royalty in my paintings. Christ is one of *us* in my pictures. In His sufferings, I want to show Him as someone who experiences and understands fully what it is like to be an unwelcome outsider.

In fairness to traditional imagery and earlier artists, Christ is an impossible figure to paint. An old friend of mine who was a Lutheran seminarian once pointed out that Christianity proclaims a 200% Christ; He is 100% human and 100% God at the same time. What in the world would such a being look like? I decided against the abstract Christ of Byzantine tradition, and more ethereal interpretations. I don't believe in flesh versus spirit dualities. The flesh informs the spirit and the spirit illumines the flesh. I wanted to make the body and flesh of Jesus teach compassion to the spirit through its suffering. I wanted that same flesh to be made radiant by the spirit at the Resurrection. I wanted a very physical and corporeal Christ, the same thing both Rubens and Rembrandt in their own very different ways tried to paint. I wanted to make him charismatic and attractive, to portray him as someone who touches and is touched, who feels pain and humiliation physically, and whose resurrection and glorification are also physical. I believe that the patient animal that is host to our souls is entitled to its dignity, and will see salvation with us in the end.

I looked to all kinds of artists for guidance and inspiration for this project. How could I not? This subject matter is central to more than a thousand years of Western art. Not only Dürer, but Giotto, Titian, Duccio, Rogier Van Der Weyden, Brueghel, Rembrandt, Bellini, Piero della Francesca, Poussin, Caravaggio, and many others inspired and guided me. I looked to artists like Goya, Blake, and more modern artists like Max Beckman, Francis Bacon, and Leon Golub. I looked at the work of photojournalists, especially at Charles Moore's photos from the Civil Rights era. I also looked to movies for guidance as well, especially the films of Orson Welles.

This project went through quite a history that bears on what it means and why I bothered to paint it in the first place. I began this series in the summer of 2001 shortly after finishing a series of paintings about the life of the artist and writer David Wojnarowicz. I had four panels completed when the events of September 11th happened. I lived in the East Village at the time and witnessed the whole catastrophe from the roof of my building. My studio was (and still is) on the Lower East Side and was inaccessible for days following the attacks. When I could finally return to my studio, after spending some time in the smoke and dust reeling from the shock of it all, I decided to concentrate exclusively on this project as a way of sorting out the issues that September 11th raised in my mind.

Most people claimed a renewal of religious faith in the wake of the September 11th attacks. I had the opposite reaction. I was horrified by the religious motivation behind the attacks and wanted nothing to do with religion at all for a little more than a year. I'm not sure the experience really changed me as much as confirmed convictions that I already held for most of my life. Pascal's words "Men never do evil so willingly or so happily than when they do it for the sake of conscience" haunted me in the days after the attack. I didn't read the Bible. I read Camus' *The Plague* in the wake of the attacks, not to "explain" any meaning, but to confirm what I saw in front of me as people responded to the disaster, and what to learn from that response. The Bible seemed to me at the time to be part of the problem, not a solution to anything.

All of my life, I've had a love-hate, on-again, off-again relationship with Christianity and with the rest of religion. I've been privileged to know some truly brave and good people, generous and even saintly people who did amazing things because of their religious convictions. I count the Reverend Barbara Crafton among those people, and I dedicated this series of paintings to her. I've known her for many years and I've seen her work with everyone from sailors to theater folk to migrant laborers in the hospitality business to the friendless and homeless. She sometimes does this work despite considerable risk to herself. I still try to comprehend how religion could include someone like Barbara Crafton together with a suicidal mass-murderer like Mohammed Atta and the rest of the killers from September 11th, 2001. I never quite solved that dilemma, and perhaps I never will. As far as I am concerned, those exemplary religious that I've known in my life, and the murderous fanatics who always cause so much grief and sorrow, inhabit different moral universes. They can only meet in the dangerous borderland where that which is immortal and unworldly bumps up against what is mortal and worldly. The Passion paintings also address the confrontation between inspiration and authority, between principle and power.

Perhaps I may justly be accused of compartmentalizing, but while I blamed religion for the 9/11 attacks and for so much crime (I do so unequivocally in the Passion paintings), I also blamed politics and human nature. I never blamed God for this. I've never believed in a controlling deity who causes everything that happens. "The God of Love will never withdraw our right to grief and infamy," said W.H. Auden. The crime was committed by a handful of homicidal fanatics, not God. I don't believe in a rescuer God either. Terrible things happen to us because we are mortal. Catastrophes have no further meaning than that. They are not punishment for any sins in this life or a past one, and they are certainly not God's will or design.

I have little love for the Christian Religion, an aggressive imperial cult with a long history of crime. But I have a deep love for the Christian Faith. I love its radicalism most of all. The very idea of

The very idea of God becoming a human being and going through everything we must go through is most revolutionary.

God becoming a human being and going through everything we must go through is most revolutionary. The religions of the world are full of gods who are murdered and rise again, from Dionysus to Osiris to the Mayan Maize God. But all of those gods are kings and heroes. None of them are quite beings like us. They certainly don't claim to be one of us. In Christ, God walked in our shoes all the way to the end. God experienced our life and mortality as one of us. He put Himself into our hands as a dependent, as we are all dependent upon each other for our lives and safety. He accepted our hate as He accepted our love. He allowed Himself to be conquered, and in doing so conquered us. The life of Jesus was no success story. He left home, lived on the road upon the charity of other people, and He died the death of a common criminal. In His death and resurrection, Christ took the whole grim algebra of power and powerlessness, success and failure by which the world has always worked, and threw it out the window. It is that profoundly egalitarian and anarchist aspect of Christianity that keeps me with it; the idea that love is the great monkey-wrench thrown into the smooth workings of our ambitions and designs for power. It is through love that we transcend history. Through love, we transcend death. We are forever liberated from the claim of a dying world upon us.

I understand and accept the hostility most gays and lesbians feel for a religion that shows them so little love and so much hate and rejection. However, I think we as gay folk are in a particularly privileged position to understand the central story of the Christian Faith. Unlike our enemies, we really have been despised and rejected, men and women of sorrow and acquainted with grief. We are a living challenge to fixed assumptions about how the world is supposed to work. Each of us is a standing rebuke to those who want to decide for everyone else what is "normal," to those who want to remake the world in their own image.

As gays and lesbians, bisexuals and transgendered, we know what it means to be singled out and excluded. We've experienced people hiding their faces from us and esteeming us not. The Way of the Cross, the Via Dolorosa, is no metaphor for a lot of us, but lived experience. Some of us walked that road all the way to the bitter end, demanding to know why God had forsaken us. David Kato, Matthew Shepard, Daniel Zamudio, Fanny Ann Eddy, Roxanne Ellis and Michele Abdill, Harvey Milk, Barry Winchell, Rebecca Wight, Brandon Teena, the victims of the Upstairs Lounge fire in New Orleans, the legions executed in Muslim and Christian nations, and thousands of other murder victims were killed because their nature made them less than fully human in the eyes of their murderers. All our murdered dead, known and unknown, are images of Christ crucified. So are the hundreds of thousands who perished in the AIDS epidemic, dying in agony and poverty while our official national policy for over a decade was to look the other way and let the disease rid the country of a nuisance population. So are the hundreds of gay and lesbian young, known and unknown, who kill themselves rather than face the horror of human hatred barreling toward them. My conception of Christ's Passion was informed by all of these, as well as those of us who continue to suffer violence and intimidation around the world. That is what I've tried to paint. ●

In Christ, God walked in our shoes
all the way to the end.
God experienced our life and mortality
as one of us.

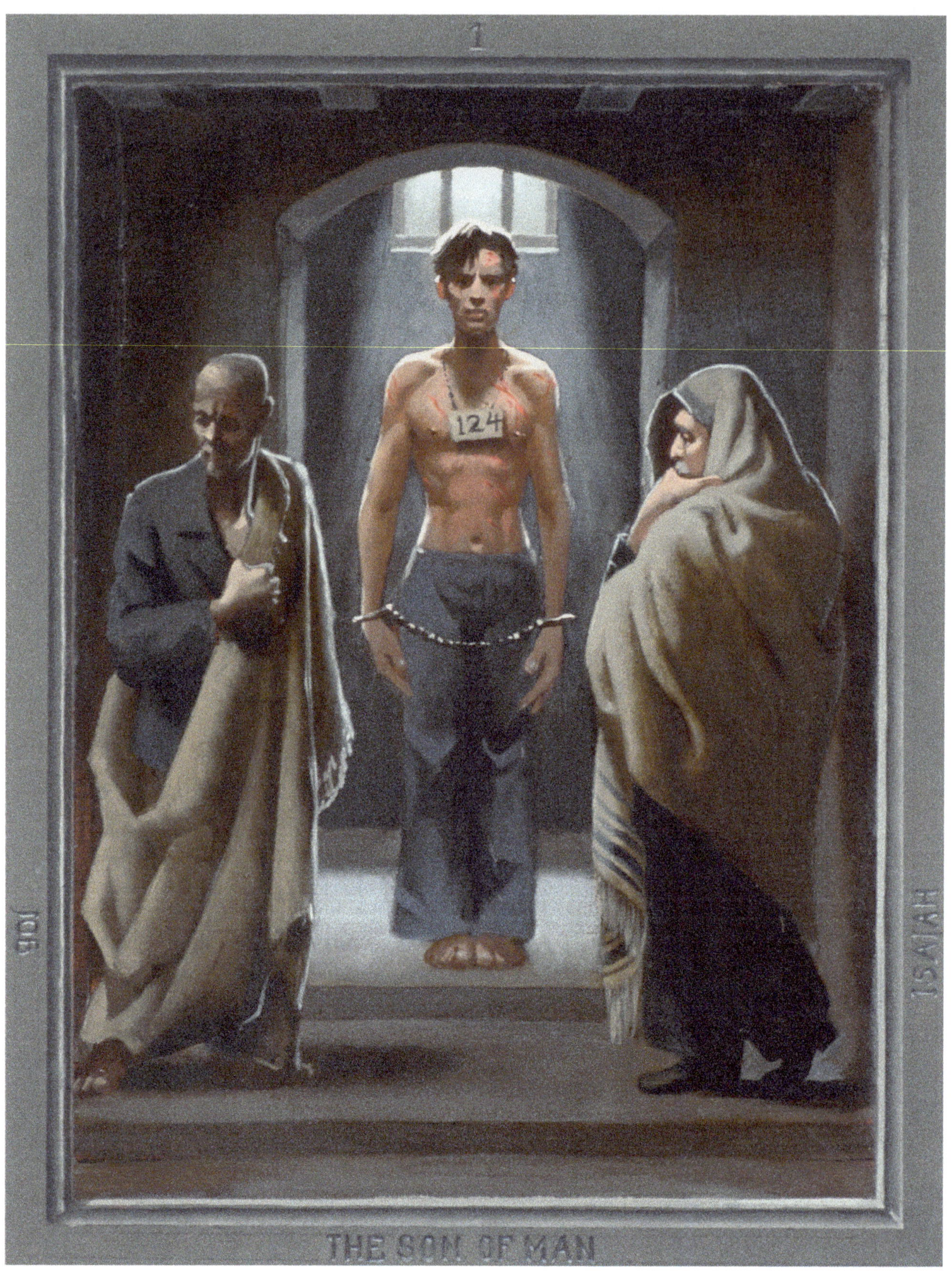

COLLECTION OF THE ARTIST

1. The Human One (Son of Man) with Job and Isaiah

"God has sent me to bind up the brokenhearted, to proclaim liberty to the captives, and the opening of the prison to those who are bound." —Isaiah 61:1*

A contemporary Jesus arrives as a prisoner in the painting that launches the series "The Passion of Christ: A Gay Vision" by Douglas Blanchard. Jesus stands half-naked in blue jeans and handcuffs, attractive even in adversity. In a modern form of dehumanization, he is labeled with a number hanging on a tag around his neck. A barred window behind an arch gives him a crude halo. His queer identity is not apparent, as often happens with contemporary lesbian, gay, bisexual, and transgender (LGBT) people. God's solidarity with people amid human suffering is emphasized from the first image in Blanchard's Passion series. Christ the liberator comes as a prisoner. With this first painting, the stage is set and the viewer is invited to join Jesus on a journey that leads from prison to paradise.

Blanchard paints an accessible Jesus that 21st-century readers can know and touch in his Passion series. The 24 paintings portray Jesus as a gay man of today in a modern city, experiencing the events of Palm Sunday, the Last Supper, and his arrest, trial, crucifixion and resurrection. The beardless young Christ is unfamiliar to modern eyes, but Blanchard harkens back to the most ancient images of Jesus. The action occurs in a generic city with a New York flavor. The gay vision of Christ's Passion promises to address the suffering of queer people today—and thereby speak to the human condition.

The pathway from bondage to freedom leads through the Passion, moving from death to new life. The word "passion" comes from the Latin word for suffering, and has become a theological term for the hardships that Jesus experienced in the week before his death. Jesus shares his dark prison cell with a pair of older men. Names painted on the sides of the frame identify his two companions as Job and

“And the Word became flesh
and dwelt among us, full of grace and truth.”
—John 1:14

Jesus was one of us, a real human being. He loved everybody, including his enemies. And yet some say that LGBT people don't belong in the story of Jesus Christ. There's black Jesus, Asian Jesus—and now gay Jesus to heal the hate and discrimination done in Christ's name. The Holy Spirit inspires each person to envision God in his or her own way. This is the story of a Jesus who emphasized his humanity by calling himself the Human One or Son of Man. He doesn't look very gay. Young and attractive, he can pass for straight. He is fully in the present, yet feels kinship with the ancient prophets Job and Isaiah, who understood suffering. He wanted to serve God by healing people and setting them free. Here we remember his last days, his death and his resurrection. Jesus was a child of God who embodied love so completely that he transcended history and even death itself. But while it was all happening, people didn't understand. Like many LGBT people, he was rejected by society. They locked the liberator in prison.

Jesus, show me how you lived and loved.

Isaiah, ancient prophets who are associated with suffering in the Hebrew scriptures. The title of this painting refers to Jesus as "Son of Man," a mysterious, multi-purpose phrase that is translated as "Human One" in gender-inclusive language.

Blanchard, a gay artist based in New York, painted this scene at the dawn of the new millennium in summer 2001. His Lower East Side studio was only two miles away from the World Trade Center. Little did he know that a few months later, on September 11, a terrorist attack there would make him confront suffering and death in a 21st-century Passion. Blanchard used the series to wrestle with his faith in the aftermath of 9/11.

The opening image is also one of the most cryptic paintings in the series. It may be tempting to skip over it and jump ahead to the next scene, where Jesus enters the city. Even the prophets turn their faces away. Job seems unable to bear seeing the bloody martyr in chains, while Isaiah appears to be lost in thought. Together the three men form a kind of Trinity. A close look reveals a surprise: The prophets of old are wearing modern suits under their robes. The lapel of a business suit is visible beneath Job's ancient garment, and the fringes of Isaiah's robe dangle over modern shoes. They present a message for today clothed in an archetypal story from long ago. Jesus faces the viewer with a full frontal gaze, ready to engage in dialogue. But he doesn't say a word. He carries nothing, no stone tablets—not even a tablet computer. Jesus himself is the message. Just by being here, he proclaims freedom.

Both Job and Isaiah are associated with suffering. Job was a righteous man who kept his faith despite horrible calamities. Throughout the whole Book of Job he wrestles with the question: Why do bad things happen to good people? A major theme in the Book of Isaiah is God's "Suffering Servant" or "Man of Sorrows" who brings justice, but is abused and rejected.

Jesus chose to quote Isaiah when he launched his public ministry. He told the people at the synagogue in Nazareth that he was fulfilling this prophecy: "The Spirit of God is upon me, because God has anointed me to preach good news to the poor, and has sent me to proclaim release to the captives and recovering of sight to the blind, to set at liberty those who are oppressed." (Luke 4:18; Isaiah 61:1) Isaiah also is known for his prophecy about a savior named Immanuel, which is Hebrew for "God with Us." Christians believe these prophecies pointed to Jesus, the godly liberator who was crucified. The New Testament describes how Christ emptied himself and took human form, living among us as the Word made flesh.

Jesus often referred to himself as "son of man," thereby emphasizing his own humanity and perhaps also invoking ancient prophecies of a messiah. By using "Son of Man" in the title, Blanchard underscores the humanity of Jesus while honoring his divinity. Jesus, Job, and Isaiah all used the phrase translated as "Son of Man" or "Human One." It can mean a generic human being (male or female) or a divine ruler envisioned by the prophet Daniel. Blanchard's choice of words reveals that this vision is progressive but not necessarily politically correct. His Jesus remains unapologetically male.

The scene of Jesus in jail with Job and Isaiah does not occur in scripture, leaving room for the viewer to speculate. Is Jesus arriving in prison or leaving? Maybe the painting represents Jesus' own vision while he prayed in prison before he was sentenced to death. He may have remembered the ancient prophets as the crowds outside shouted for his death—just a week after they roared their approval when he entered the city. Or does the picture show how society locks away today's prophets along with those of the past?

The prison scene is an enigmatic prelude for the "gay vision" proclaimed in the subtitle of the series. Americans have been imprisoned for homosexual acts within living memory. The last sodomy laws in the United States were not overturned until 2003. Consensual homosexual acts remain a crime in many countries and a few still impose the death penalty. Many queers still imprison themselves in self-imposed mental closets.

Jesus in modern dress may come as a surprise, but he promised his disciples, "Lo, I am with you always."

Early Christian artists commonly pictured Jesus as a youthful Good Shepherd without a beard. The bearded Christ motif developed around the sixth century. The crucifixion images that dominate current Christian thought didn't arise until a thousand years after he died. A Jesus in modern dress may come as a surprise, but he promised his disciples, "Lo, I am with you always" (Matthew 28:20).

Artists almost never portray Jesus in prison. A rare exception is 19th-century French painter James Tissot. He painted Jesus with hands lifted in prayer, chained to a stone between two sleeping guards in *Good Friday Morning: Jesus in Prison.* Likewise Belgian surrealist Rene Magritte is one of the few artists in history who ever attempted to give visual form to the phrase "Son of Man." His famous *Son of Man* is a self-portrait of the artist in a suit with an oversized apple covering his face.

The gay Passion series operates on two levels as a story within a story. The first and last paintings function as bookends, holding the gospel narrative in a larger context not limited by time and space. For those who take time to decode the rich symbolism of this painting, it foreshadows and sums up the whole series. This will be no ordinary Stations of the Cross, with a hopelessly distant Jesus moving predictably from trial to tomb. Blanchard's vision is broader. With this first painting, Blanchard honors human suffering by invoking major Biblical models of Christ: the Son of Man / Human One, the Suffering Servant, and Immanuel. As the averted eyes of Job and Isaiah indicate, many prophets desired to see the freedom embodied by Christ, but did not. Viewers of Blanchard's Passion are blessed with the chance to see it played out as the gay vision unfolds. ●

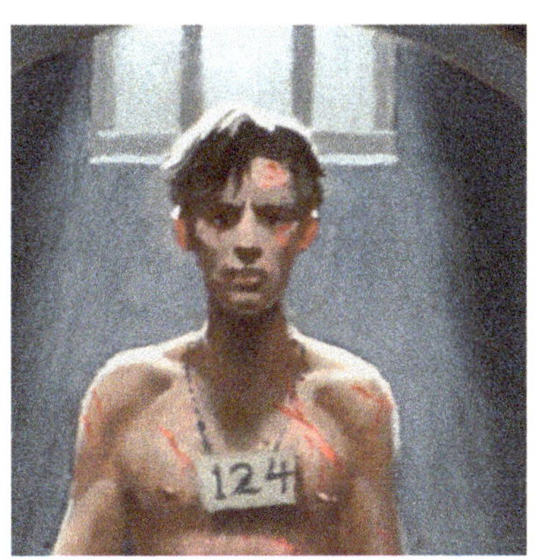
124

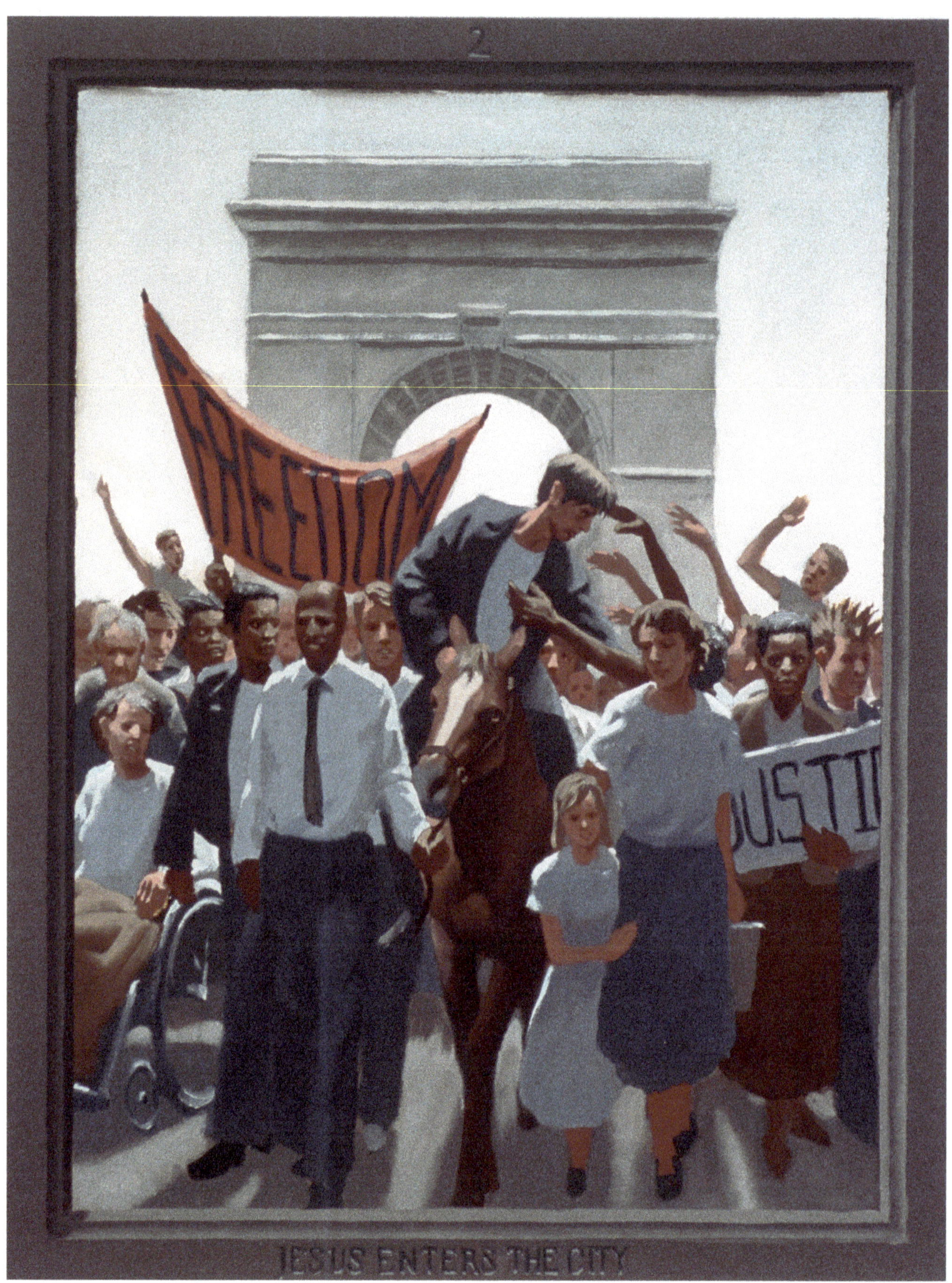

COLLECTION OF BRUCE GOERLICH

2. Jesus Enters the City

"And when he entered Jerusalem, all the city was stirred, saying, 'Who is this?' And the crowds said, 'This is the prophet Jesus.'" —Matthew 21:10-11

A diverse 21st-century crowd marches under an arch with a charismatic young man in *Jesus Enters the City*. Signs for "freedom" and "justice" make it a rally for almost any cause, from marriage equality and LGBT rights to the Occupy movement or the Tea Party. The masses adore Jesus as if he was a rock star or political leader. They stretch their hands up to him, grasping for the savior that they expect him to be. Jesus has brought together a varied group: male and female, multi-racial, young and old, queer and straight, able-bodied and wheelchair-bound. A mother and daughter lead the way, along with a black man who holds the reins of the horse that Jesus rides. By passing through the arch, Jesus leaves his old life behind to meet the new challenges ahead.

Arms raised, the people rejoice, but the sky is grey and they are not united. Their signs droop or get blocked, making them hard to read. Each person looks in a different direction, never making eye contact. As the Passion story begins, Jesus seems disconnected from the passions he stirs in others. The seeds of conflict are already planted. In the middle of this "triumph," Jesus bends down to be embraced by someone unnoticed and out of view. He is focused on something that others ignore. The crowd marches forward, about to step right out of the picture frame. The viewer can't see what Jesus sees, and the oncoming group will force viewers to make a decision: join in, back off, or get trampled underfoot. Light from the arch forms a lopsided halo behind his head.

There are no palms in Blanchard's generic cityscape, but this is an updated vision of Palm Sunday, which commemorates Jesus' entry into Jerusalem. All four gospels describe how Jesus entered Roman-occupied Jerusalem at the height of his popularity. Enthusiastic fans greeted him by laying palm branches on the ground before him and shouting "Hosanna," which translates as "Save us now!" Huge crowds were gathering in Jerusalem for the Jewish festival of Passover. They saw Jesus as a political deliverer who came to fulfill the ancient prophecies of a messiah: an earthly king anointed by God. His arrival on a donkey reminded them of the victory processions of ancestral kings descended from David. By riding a lowly donkey instead of a war horse, he hinted that he came in peace. They mistakenly thought that Jesus was declaring himself king of Israel, ready to lead a rebellion against the Roman army. Palm Sunday hints at the tradeoffs that people make in pursuit of power. As the crowds marched into Jerusalem with Jesus, they were already on the path that would lead to his destruction. Their movement was gaining momentum on a trajectory that could not be altered or stopped. "If these were silent, the very stones would cry out," (Luke 19:40) Jesus told the traditionalists who wanted him to quiet the crowd.

Jesus' triumphant entry foreshadows the emptiness and impermanence of earthly glory. Luke's gospel says that Jesus wept over the city when his procession got close to Jerusalem, the center of Jewish religious and national life. More than once in the Bible he lamented over Jerusalem's inability to recognize God's prophets. He longed to gather its people together "as a hen gathers her brood under her wings," but they refused. Jesus signaled a power not of this world, while they sought worldly power. He was surrounded by adoring crowds on the way to Jerusalem, but they were not the true community that would be forged by the hardships ahead. Every hero's journey begins with entry into a new place. On Palm Sunday Jesus leaves behind his old life as an itinerant teacher and healer, crossing through a gateway to face death itself for the good of all.

Crowd scenes are one of Blanchard's strengths as an artist. He makes fine use of that talent in *Jesus Enters the City,* which is one of the most popular images in his whole Passion series. He can capture a crowd's unruly movements almost like a stop-action camera. Indeed while working on this series, the artist studied Charles Moore's photos of the American civil rights movement. Blanchard paints each face in the crowd as a unique individual. For example the young man in a spiky mohawk carrying the "justice" sign on the right looks like he just stepped out of a LGBT Pride march. Most artists from history have shown Jesus marching through the gate in profile or three-quarter view, but Blanchard takes the unusual step of making Jesus head straight at the viewer.

Jesus' entry into Jerusalem is one of the oldest Christian images. It can be found among the earliest Christian artworks in the Catacombs of Rome, where the fourth-century sarcophagus of Junius Bassus shows Jesus riding into Jerusalem on a donkey. The image follows a tradition in Roman Imperial art of depicting the formal arrival (*adventus*) of the emperor into a city during or after a military campaign. Christ entering Jerusalem has been portrayed by many great artists from the Middle Ages to the Baroque era. One of the oldest and best-known versions is a fresco painted by Giotto in 1305 at the Arena Chapel in Padua. German Renaissance artist Albrecht Dürer engraved it in his Small Passion series, which Blanchard acknowledges as a source for his gay vision of the Passion. But the scene is

“Look, the world has gone after him.”

—John 12:19

Everyone cheered when Jesus called for justice and freedom. Crowds followed him into the city, shouting and waving. Their chants were not so different from ours: “Yes we can! Out of the closet and into the streets! We’re here, we’re queer, get used to it!” Jesus was a superstar making a grand entrance. But he did it in his own modest, gentle style. He surprised people by riding on a donkey. Some of his supporters, those who had mainstream success, urged him to quiet the others—assimilate, don’t alienate. Tone it down. Act respectable, don’t demand respect. Stop flaunting it. His answer: I’m here to liberate people! If the crowds were silent, the stones would cry out! It was that kind of day, a Palm Sunday sort of day, when everyone shouted for equality and freedom. But was anybody still listening?

Hey, Jesus, here I am!

omitted from the traditional Stations of the Cross, which instead starts days later when Jesus is condemned to death. Modern artists have mostly ignored Palm Sunday in favor of other episodes from the life of Christ. An exception is Swedish photographer Elisabeth Ohlson Wallin. She reenvisioned Jesus' life in a contemporary LGBT setting with the notorious 1998 series named *Ecce Homo*. Her version of the arrival in Jerusalem shows Jesus riding a bicycle in Stockholm's festive LGBT Pride Parade.

Triumphal arches were invented by the ancient Romans and remain one of their most influential architectural forms. The arch in this painting is a simplified version of the Washington Square Arch in New York City, where Blanchard has lived since 1991. It is a landmark in Greenwich Village, an artsy neighborhood with a nonconformist tradition. That arch was in turn based on the first-century Arch of Titus in Rome, which also inspired the Arc de Triomphe in Paris. The Arch of Titus was built to commemorate the siege of Jerusalem, yet ironically in this painting it serves as the gateway to Jerusalem for the doomed Jesus. The Arc de Triomphe played a role in military victory rallies for rulers from Napoleon to Hitler. In 1999 a new version aggrandized a contemporary kind of empire: a Las Vegas casino. All of these arches stand for material power, and thereby hint at its transience as times change.

Arriving in a city is often an LGBT rite of passage.

Arriving in a city is often an LGBT rite of passage. Many queer people leave their homes to find freedom in an urban mecca where they congregate and form their own communities. Marching in an LGBT Pride parade for the first time is an experience not unlike Jesus' triumphal entry. Pride marches celebrate LGBT culture and serve as demonstrations for equal rights. Like Jesus' arrival in Jerusalem, Pride parades are raucous, wildly joyful celebrations—and they can mask potential hazards. The LGBT community is not immune from the dangers that have plagued underprivileged groups since before Jesus' time: In the quest to gain political power, communities can lose touch with the true power that they already have through their unique culture, spirituality, shared history, and connection with each other. Hostile outside forces can take advantage of internal divisions to crush any leaders who rise up to defy the system.

Palm Sunday marks the beginning of Holy Week, a period of reflection on Christ's Passion leading up to Easter. With this second painting in the series, Blanchard dives into the ambitious project of telling the Passion story in a contemporary urban setting from a gay perspective. The action will not stop until the final painting. Let the adventure begin! ●

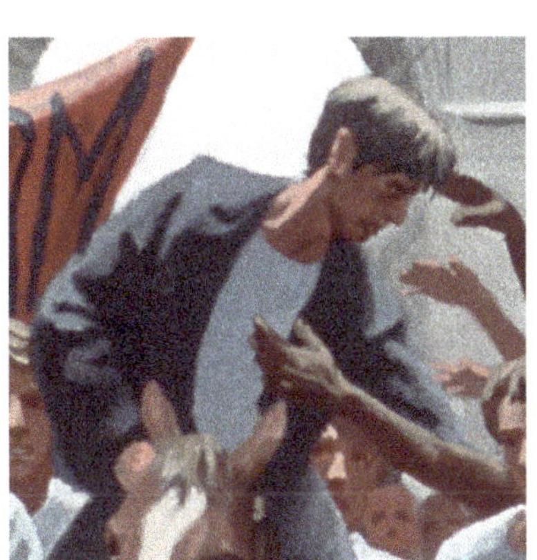

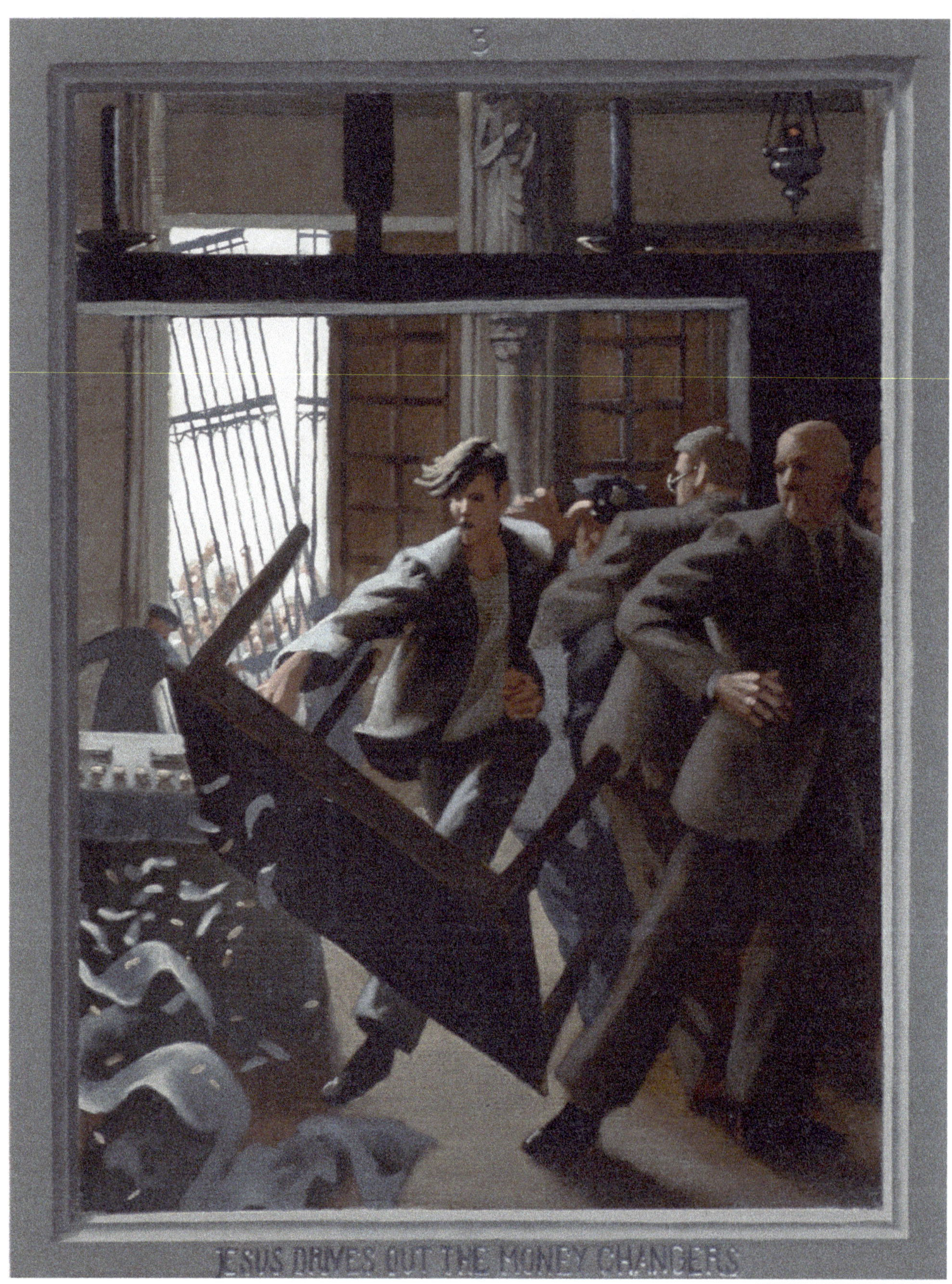

COLLECTION OF THE ARTIST

3. Jesus Drives Out the Money Changers

"He poured out the coins of the money-changers and overturned their tables." —John 2:15

An angry young man disrupts business in *Jesus Drives Out the Money Changers*. Jesus, hair flying, overturns tables stacked with money. Coins scatter, bills flutter away, and the men in suits run. A crowd in the background yanks off the barred gate that separates them from the wealthy money managers. One security guard struggles to keep out the mob. Another officer reaches to grab Jesus by the shoulder. Jesus looks like a freedom fighter standing up against greed and income inequality. The protest resembles a scene from Occupy Wall Street, although it was painted a decade before that movement began. The setting appears to be a present-day bank, church office, or other financial institution with statues, classic columns, and a hanging lamp.

All four gospels describe what is commonly called "the cleansing of the temple." By some accounts Jesus kicked the money changers out of the temple as soon as he arrived in Jerusalem. When he saw them taking advantage of people's faith in God, he exploded. It was the only time that Jesus used physical violence in the Bible. Jesus poured out the coins of the money changers and turned over their tables. Then he made a whip of cords and used it to chase them out, along with the sacrificial animals that they were selling. He yelled, "My house shall be called a house of prayer, but you make it a den of robbers." It was one of many occasions when he blasted religious leaders for exploiting the poor in the name of God. He understood the importance of economic issues. Jesus talked more about money than anything else except God.

Blanchard is correct to paint the cleansing in a place that could be either a bank or a church because the temple in Jerusalem was not only

"It is written, 'My house shall be called a house of prayer,'
but you make it a den of robbers." —Matthew 21:13

Jesus acted up when he saw something wrong. Nothing made him angrier than religious hypocrisy blocking the way to God. He got mad when religious leaders made people pay to attend worship. He said, you can't buy your way to heaven! Everyone gets God for free. Don't trick a poor widow into giving her last penny! The sacrifice that pleases God is to do justice and love people. Oh sure, you can raise tons of money by claiming that some other group is an unholy threat: lepers, immigrants, queers. Stop demonizing people! You call gays an abomination, but your fundraising tactics are the real abomination! Hypocrites! You're like fancy tombs, pretty on the outside, but full of death on the inside. Then he turned over the tables where the men in suits made their unholy profits. Coins went flying as he drove them out.

Jesus, thank you for your anger.
Give me the courage to act up against injustice.

a religious institution, but also functioned as a national bank. The temple held private deposits of wealth in its treasury, made loans, and collected debts, as well as selling animals for sacrifice. The money changers of first-century Jerusalem exchanged foreign currency for the temple coins that were required for paying the annual temple tax and making offerings. They made big profits by using unfair exchange rates and adding service charges. Priests also got a cut.

Jesus' rant and rampage against the money changers has fascinated artists since the Middle Ages. Their paintings of the episode go by various names, such as the purification of the temple, the expulsion of the money changers, or driving the merchants from the temple. Renaissance master El Greco painted at least five versions. But overall the angry outburst has been downplayed in favor of the other events from the life of a more passive Christ. Modern artists mostly ignore the subject.

Blanchard is perhaps the only artist to paint a "gay vision" of the day that Jesus fought back against the merchants who turned the holy temple into a marketplace. His Jesus could be upset about the growing gap between the wealthy one percent and the other 99 percent, or about fundraising tactics that demonize LGBT people, or about countless other forms of economic injustice. ●

Jesus' rampage against the money changers has fascinated artists since the Middle Ages.

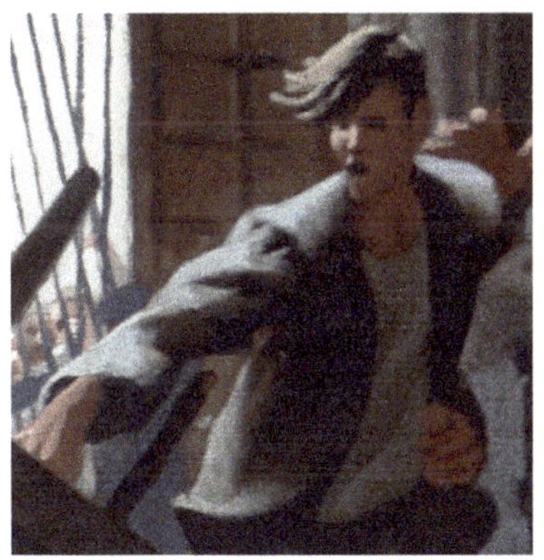

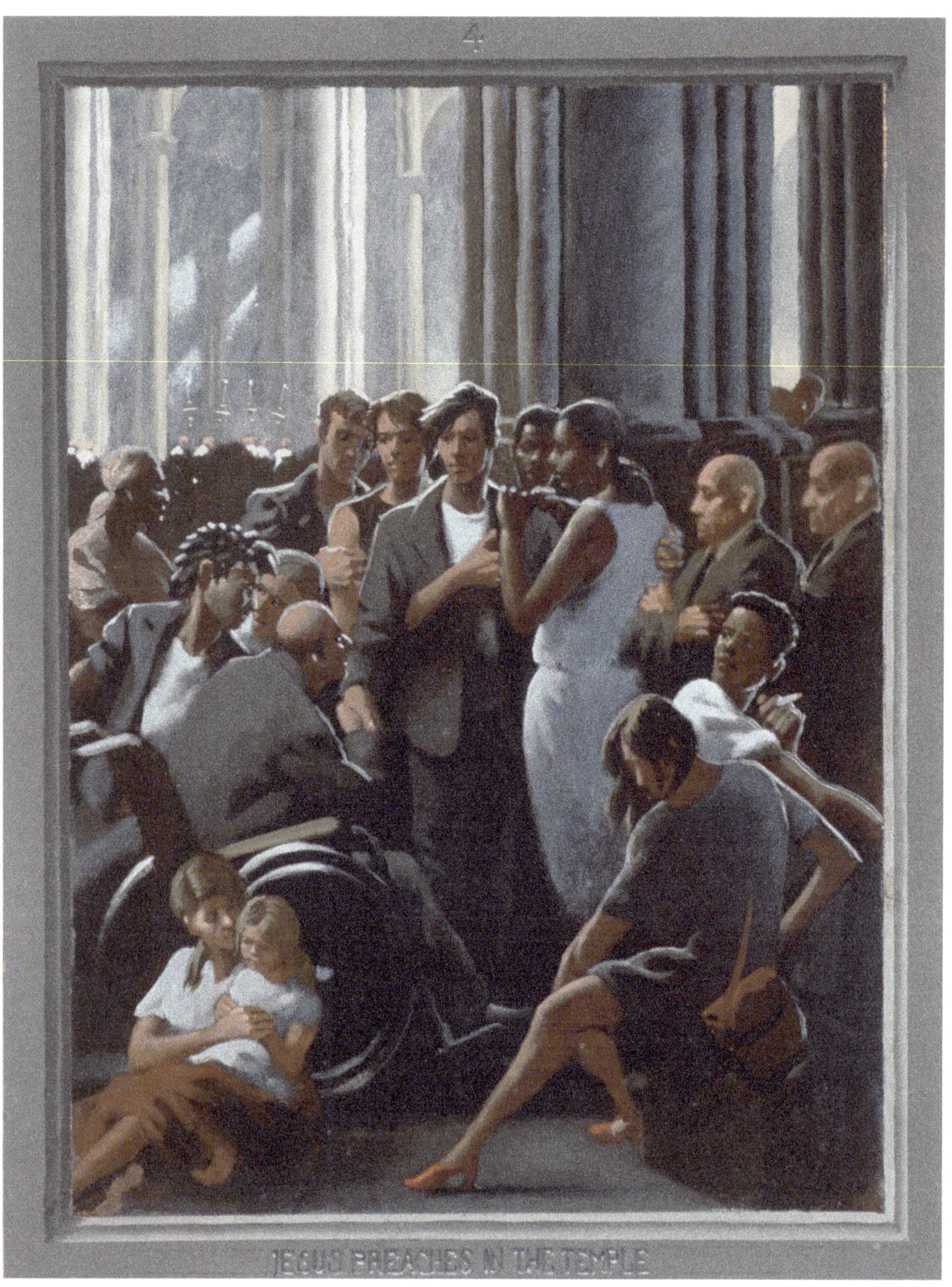

COLLECTION OF THE ARTIST

4. Jesus Preaches in the Temple

"The chief priests...feared him, because all the multitude was astonished at his teaching."
—Mark 11:18

A popular teacher distracts churchgoers from a worship service in *Jesus Preaches in the Temple*. Jesus, looking like an urban hipster, welcomes the people who crowd around and touch him. The title states that Jesus is preaching, but he stands quietly among them, mouth closed, communicating compassion with his presence. Blue tones conjure a peaceful mood, but there is tension between the upstart preacher and the religious establishment, between the individual and the institution.

This painting raises the question: What would happen if Jesus walked into a church of today? The general consensus is that he would disrupt the established order. Not many Christians would stay meekly in their pews and settle for stale sermons and wafers if they had the chance to see, hear, and touch the living Christ. Those who gain power by speaking for Jesus might prefer to keep him away.

The individualized faces and gestures of Jesus' listeners invite speculation about their lives. Two gay couples wrap Jesus in a loving embrace: a white couple on the left and a black couple on the right. Jesus puts his arm around one of the black men while shaking hands with—and perhaps healing—the bald man in the wheelchair. Even cool guys are drawn to Jesus: one with a spiky mohawk hairdo and another smoking a cigarette. Others sit in front, just wanting to be near Jesus: a mother and daughter on the left, and on the right a downcast figure in red high heels. Her tall, awkward body suggests a drag queen or a transgender woman.

Large pillars and arches hint that they are in the aisle of a modern cathedral. Far in the distance on the left, a row of priests carries candles or shiny processional crosses, as happens in a contemporary cathedral during worship.

The two-fold message that the Biblical Jesus taught was love and justice.

But many congregants are more interested in Jesus. A man peeks around the pillar on the back right to see who is causing all the excitement.

Not everyone is pleased to see the charismatic newcomer. Two bald men eavesdrop, arms crossed. Their suits suggest that they are businessmen, but they could easily be church bureaucrats. They look like the money changers who were attacked by Jesus in the previous painting. This ominous pair might even be another gay couple, but a conservative and perhaps closeted duo with a stake in the status quo. Whatever their identity, they are the modern counterparts of the elders, scribes, lawyers, priests, and Pharisees in the Bible who observed Jesus in the temple, looking for a way to destroy him.

It's possible to guess what Jesus might be saying in this painting by reading the lengthy Biblical accounts of his preaching. The two-fold message that the Biblical Jesus taught was love and justice. Blanchard's *Jesus Preaches in the Temple* counterbalances the previous image of Jesus driving out the money changers. He stood for justice against the money changers before, and here he stands for love. The Bible records much of what Jesus taught, but he himself said the most important lesson was this: Love God with all your heart, and love your neighbor as yourself.

Images of Jesus preaching or teaching in the temple are relatively rare in art history. Even Renaissance master Albrecht Dürer, whose Small Passion contains no less than 38 engravings, did not include such a scene. The drama of Jesus' crucifixion tends to overshadow the content of his teachings, but Blanchard reminds viewers that Christ illumined the world not just by the way he died, but by how he lived and what he taught.

One subject that Jesus never discussed directly was homosexuality. He certainly didn't condemn it in the Bible. He may even have implied that LGBT people are born that way when he said, "There are eunuchs who have been so from birth." (Matthew 19:12) Some progressive Bible scholars believe that Jesus used an ancient term for LGBT people when he talked about eunuchs. The term translated as "eunuch" probably included not just castrated men, but also a variety of sexual minorities that today would be called LGBT or queer. ●

“All the people hung upon his words.” —Luke 19:48

All kinds of people crowded around Jesus: male and female, young and old, rich and poor, healthy and sick, people from every race and nation—and the queer ones: women who acted like men, men who acted like women, those who loved someone of the same sex, those with bodies somewhere between male and female. People lumped all of the queers together and called them “eunuchs.” Jesus said some were born eunuchs, some were made into eunuchs by others, and some made themselves into eunuchs. He never spoke a word against homosexuality. He just taught about love. Religious leaders felt threatened by his absolute love, but his words and his actions touched and healed people: “Love God with all your strength, love your neighbor as yourself, love your enemies.” The religious leaders listened too—hoping he would say something that they could use to silence him.

Jesus, teach me, touch me!

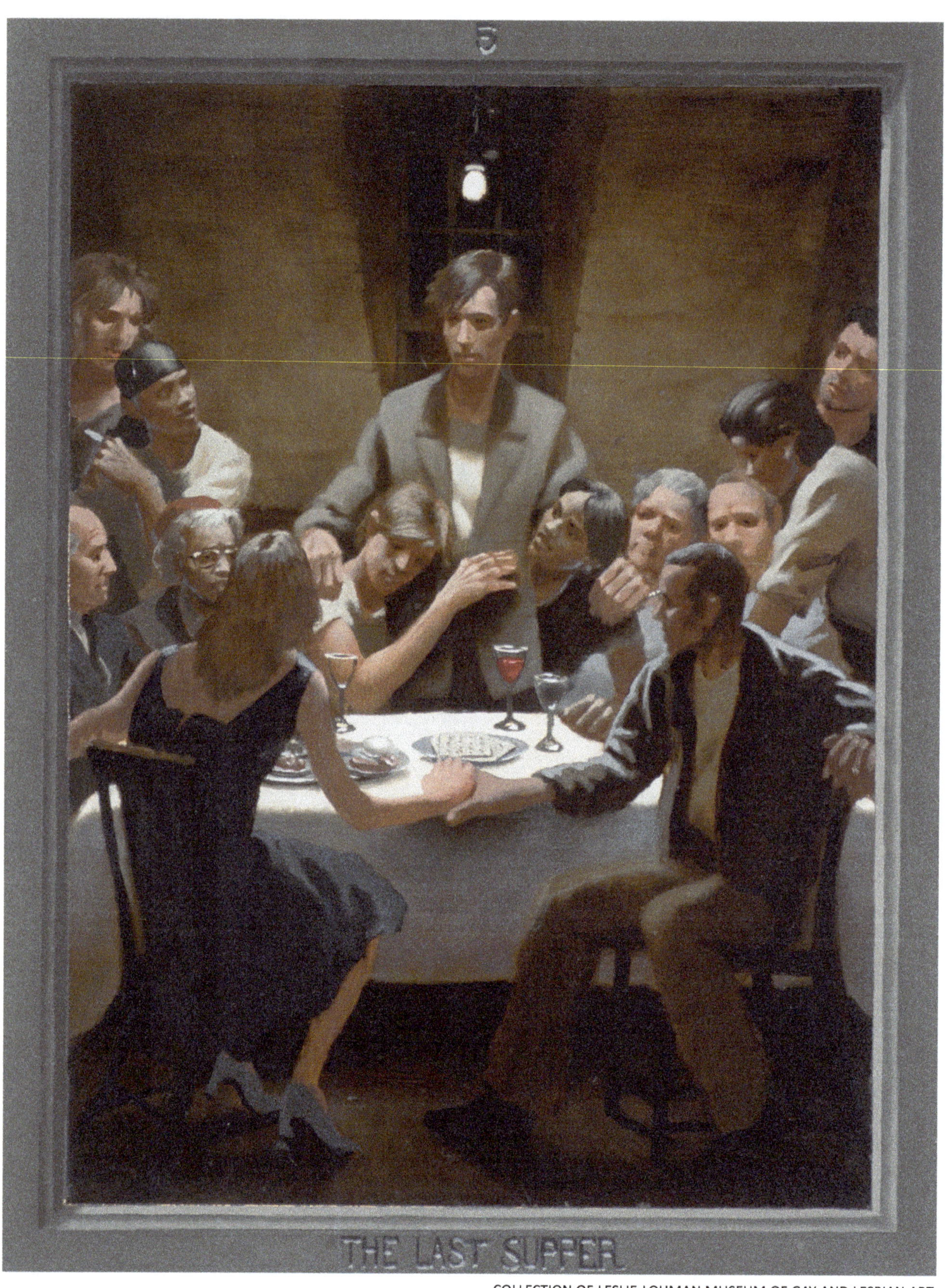

COLLECTION OF LESLIE-LOHMAN MUSEUM OF GAY AND LESBIAN ART
GIFT OF VINCENT PALANGE IN MEMORY OF LOUIS PRUDENTI (ID NUMBER 2004.2847.0001)

5. The Last Supper

"And during supper...one of his disciples, whom Jesus loved,
was lying close to the breast of Jesus." —John 13:2, 23

Friends get together for an intimate dinner in *The Last Supper*. The contemporary Christ figure dines with twelve people, the classic dozen disciples, but they are a multi-racial group of many ages, sexual orientations, and gender identities. An elderly black woman sits beside a white businessman. A drag queen in high heels holds hands with a man. The face of Jesus looks almost the same as when he was preaching in the temple... impassive. He wraps his arms around the men beside him. The whole group is joined by touch, and yet they are not completely united. They express emotions ranging from surprise to sorrow, and each one looks in a different direction. Plates hold food for a Passover Seder meal, including matzo bread, a hard-boiled egg, and roast lamb. A single glass of blood-red wine stands out against the drab colors, hinting at the sacrifice to come. The room is simple, lit only by a bare light bulb. They are seated in a way that invites the viewer to join them at the table.

All four gospels describe the final meal that Jesus ate with his disciples before he was arrested. Biblical accounts of the Last Supper are full of dramatic details and dialogue, making it possible to imagine much of what happened on that fateful night. Jesus announced to his startled disciples that one of them would betray him. They were shocked again when he identified the bread and wine as his own body and blood, urging them to eat and drink their share of it. In giving new meaning to the Passover meal, he helped prepare them for his impending death. He summarized his teachings on love and gave them a new commandment: Love each other as I have loved you. He prayed for believers in the present and future.

“This is my body which is given for you.
Do this in remembrance of me.” —Luke 22:19

Jesus' friends didn't know it would be their last meal with him, even though he tried to prepare them. All his closest friends were there, including the man whom Jesus loved. Jesus snuggled his beloved and talked about love, and then about betrayal, and then a lot more about love. Jesus said he was going away and urged them all to love each other as he had loved them. The greatest love, he told them, is to lay down your life for your friends. He handed bread to them and said something totally unexpected: Take, eat; this is my body. Then he passed around a cup, saying, Drink, all of you, this is my blood. He gave and they received completely, an act of true communion. The wine tasted sweet, with a touch of bitterness.

Jesus, thank you for feeding me!

> The man leaning his head on Jesus must be the unnamed "disciple whom Jesus loved."

He told them that the greatest love is to lay down your life for your friends.

By inviting his friends to remember him whenever they shared bread and cup, Jesus instituted a sacrament and invested all meals with a living sense of God's presence. Christians relive the Last Supper every time they celebrate the ritual known as the Eucharist, Holy Communion, or the Lord's Supper. The sacred meal is a central act of worship in which believers remember Jesus and ingest God's spirit. In Blanchard's painting, one glass is still full of wine, meaning that Jesus hasn't yet passed it to his friends, saying, "This cup is the new covenant in my blood."

The man leaning his head on Jesus must be the unnamed "disciple whom Jesus loved." The beloved disciple is referenced five times in the gospel of John. The term implies that Jesus was in love with him, and for centuries some interpreters have suggested they had a homosexual relationship. The Bible states that the beloved rested his head on Jesus' chest at the Last Supper. Blanchard puts them in a pose that echoes medieval paintings and sculptures, such as the 14th-century German *Johannesminne* (John Love) by the Master of Oberschwaben. Their same-sex attraction has been spotlighted by today's LGBT-affirming artists and Bible scholars, but here their relationship blends naturally into the group. Some also enjoy speculating about the homoerotic undertones of the relationship between Jesus and Judas, the disciple who betrayed him. But that is not Blanchard's focus. It's not even possible to identify Judas in his Last Supper.

The Last Supper is one of the most popular (and most often parodied) subjects in art. Artists usually focus on either the announcement of the betrayal or else, like Blanchard, on the institution of the Eucharist. Depictions of the Last Supper date back to the earliest Christian frescoes in the second-century Catacombs of Rome, although some scholars say the supper scenes in the Catacombs show a future meal in heaven promised by Christ. For the first thousand years of Christian history, artists tended to skip from the Last Supper to the resurrection. The Eucharist was celebrated as a feast of life instead of a re-enactment of his death. The bread and wine were not the crucified Christ, but the resurrected Christ. By the Renaissance it had become a favorite subject. Leonardo Da Vinci's Last

Supper from the 1490s continues to be one of the most famous paintings of all time. It has sparked a seemingly endless variety of imitations, from the sublime to the ridiculous. Some use it to make political statements, such as the all-female *Yo Mama's Last Supper* by Jamaican-American artist Renee Cox and "The First Supper" by Susan Dorothea White of Australia. Modern interpretations of the Last Supper have been done by many renowned artists, including Salvador Dali, who used surrealism and symmetry to portray the mystical meal.

By presenting a complex, up-to-date vision of the Last Supper, Blanchard makes room for viewers to inhabit a scene that may have grown monotonous from over-familiarity. Artists such as Elisabeth Ohlson Wallin and Becki Jayne Harrelson have created queer versions of the Last Supper by duplicating DaVinci's famous composition and replacing the characters with contemporary LGBT people. Blanchard goes further to re-conceive the whole composition. His queer elements include not only the beloved disciple, but also a drag queen in high heels. He puts her right up front as a courtesy. But his Last Supper is not an LGBT-only party. Queers are integrated into a mixed group. Jesus welcomes all kinds of people at the sacred meal where friends are invited to "do this in remembrance of me." ●

Jesus welcomes
all kinds
of people
at the
sacred meal.

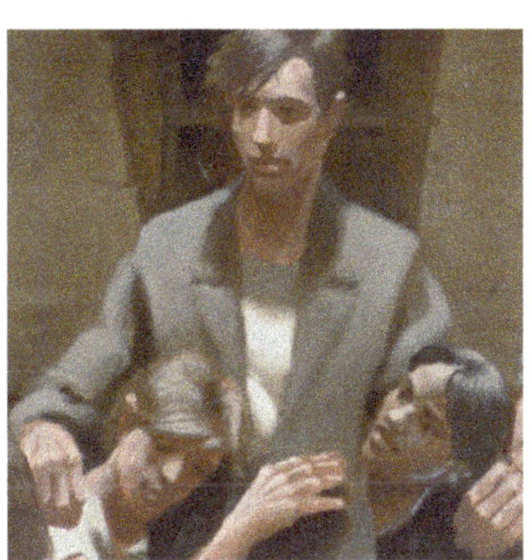

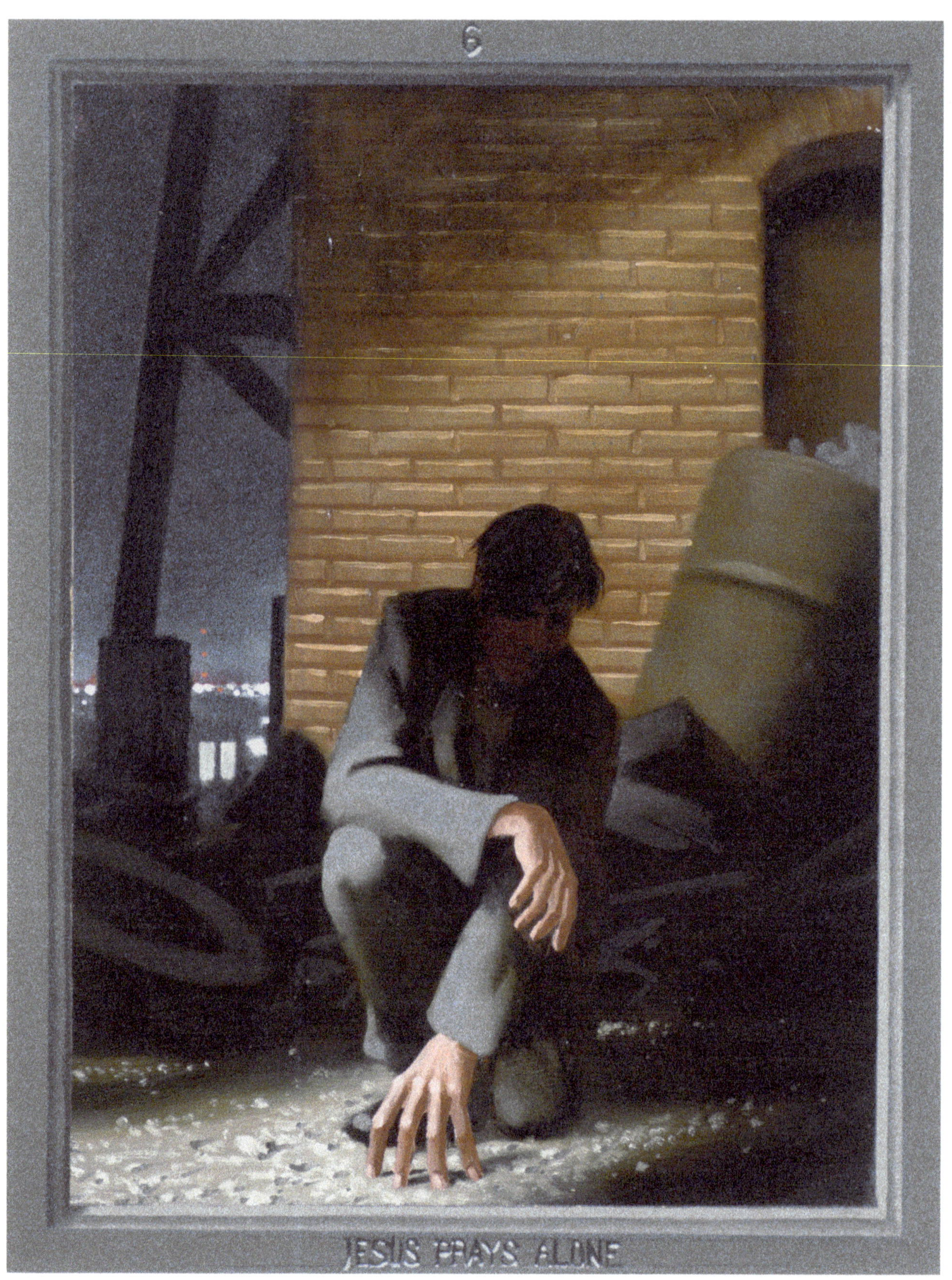

COLLECTION OF PAUL BRIDGEWATER

6. Jesus Prays Alone

"And being in an agony he prayed more earnestly." —Luke 22:44

A man claws the ground with gut-wrenching spiritual torment in *Jesus Prays Alone*. His face is lost in darkness—he could be anyone—but his tortured hand is spotlighted front and center in stark relief. Jesus kneels, utterly alone, on a rooftop with trash cans and brick walls. This is the modern Gethsemane—not a garden, but an urban jungle where a lone man wrestles with an impossible dilemma: betray his own beliefs or die. City lights glimmer against the night sky.

The simplicity of the image makes an immediate impact. It is the only painting in Blanchard's Passion series where Jesus is alone. Even in death Jesus is with other corpses, but here everyone has deserted him, and God is not visible. The solitude is absolute. The painting stuns many viewers more than the explicitly violent scenes ahead. The artist captures Christ's emotional distress and makes it up close and personal, leaving the viewer alone with Jesus. Blanchard borrows the high-contrast lighting, grim urban setting, and fatalistic mood from film noir, making an almost cinematic statement.

In the Bible, Jesus and his friends went to the secluded garden of Gethsemane after the Last Supper. He confided that he felt "deeply grieved, even to death" and asked his friends to pray with him, but they all fell asleep. Jesus knew that his ministry had brought him into conflict with authorities who would arrest and kill him. He was so upset that some ancient authorities say he sweated blood. And yet he chose not to escape the harrowing journey ahead. The doomed prophet would not deny what he believed by running away to hide. Forsaken by his sleepy friends, he was left alone to beg God over and over: "If possible, please remove this cup from me: yet, not what

The Gethsemane scene can symbolize any spiritual anguish, including the struggles of LGBT people.

I want, but what you want." The episode establishes that Jesus is not God's puppet or a victim of circumstances, but a free agent making his own moral decisions.

Jesus Prays Alone marks a turning point in Blanchard's own relationship to the Passion series, which he began painting in summer 2001. He had finished four panels by Sept. 11 when hijacked planes crashed into the World Trade Center near his studio on New York's Lower East Side. He watched the terrorist attacks in shock from the roof of his apartment building in the East Village. Horrified by the religious motive for the 9/11 attacks, Blanchard became alienated from religion. The artist acknowledges that he began to use the Passion series to resolve his spiritual conflict. In the sixth panel Jesus, with his own rooftop agony, takes on the sorrows that stretch to the 21st century.

Artists mostly ignored the scene of Jesus' inner turmoil until the rise of individualism in the Renaissance. Then the subject, often called "The Agony in the Garden," became increasingly popular. A notable modern version was painted by French Post-Impressionist Paul Gauguin, whose poignant self-portrait in *Christ in the Garden of Olives* expresses his own pain over crushed ideals.

The Gethsemane scene can symbolize any spiritual anguish, including the struggles of LGBT people to reconcile their sexuality with their religion, to live as whole human beings even when church and society label them sinful or sick. In a world that often denies the value of queer lives, many LGBT people have felt utterly alone, trapped between denying themselves and confronting the "social death" of persecution and exclusion. Crouching in a back alley, the Jesus of today could be praying for an end to the suffering of God's queer children. ●

"He fell on the ground and prayed that,

if it were possible, the hour might pass from him." —Mark 14:35

After supper, Jesus and his friends went to an isolated place. Jesus wanted to pray alone. He asked his friends to wait and pray nearby. He knew that his actions—even his very existence—brought him into inevitable conflict with authorities who wanted him dead. His wildly inclusive way of loving challenged the power structures and the status quo. But he could not deny who God created him to be. He wouldn't stop loving. He couldn't. He had to be true to himself. Authorities would condemn him as a sinner because his love broke all the rules. They would denounce his love as sin. They might even kill him. Jesus prayed in agony: God, if it's possible, let this cup pass by me. I don't want to drink it. Nevertheless, not my will, but yours be done.

Guide me, God! I put my life in your hands.

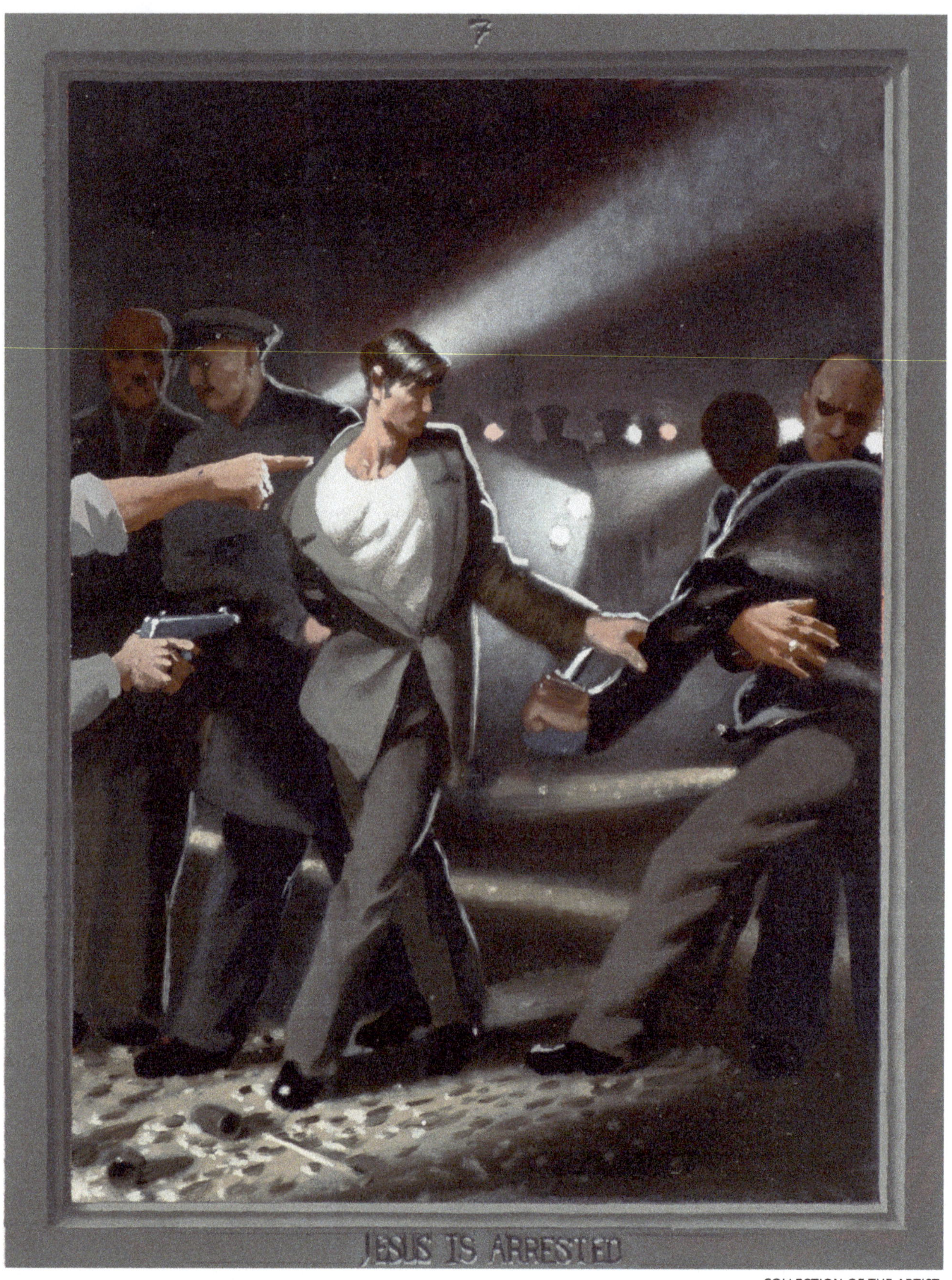

COLLECTION OF THE ARTIST

7. Jesus is Arrested

"Have you come out as against a robber, with swords and clubs to capture me?"

—Matthew 26:55

A young suspect stops his friends from fighting back when officers seize him in *Jesus is Arrested.* A disembodied hand points an accusing finger at Jesus from the left. Another hand aims a gun at him. A friend starts to defend him with a knife, but Jesus prevents him. Flashlight beams and searchlights pierce the urban night, forming a partial halo behind Jesus' head. Standing in the background, shrouded by darkness, is a bald man in a suit, probably one of the creeps who spied on Jesus at the temple. Dark silhouettes on the horizon show that many more guards and police are on the way. Jesus is caught off-balance in the cross of an X-shaped composition, adding to the dramatic tension.

The painting captures the moment when Jesus meets hate with love by submitting to the unjustified arrest. Blanchard strips the scene of sentimentality by presenting it with gritty realism. The image gets a film-noir vibe from its stark black-and-white lighting and the sense that an innocent man is caught in a deadly web.

The arrest of Jesus is a pivotal scene that ends his public ministry and begins the chain of events leading to his execution. The gospels describe the action in quick succession: The traitor Judas arrives with a large squad of police, guards, and soldiers, armed to the teeth with far more swords and clubs than necessary. Judas kisses Jesus as a signal identifying him to the soldiers. Another disciple counterattacks, swinging a sword to cut off the ear of the high priest's servant. Jesus commands his companions to put away their weapons. The soldiers seize Jesus and bind him. His disciples flee. A young man follows wearing only a linen cloth. The soldiers grab him, but he pulls free and he runs away naked. They lead Jesus to the high priest.

"Put your sword back into its place; for all who take the sword will perish by the sword." —Matthew 26:52

Jesus didn't try to escape when the police and soldiers came for him in the dead of night. He and his friends were used to police harassment and government persecution. Authorities tend to pick on the poorest, queerest, and most marginalized in any society. This time they came out in force, like a small army with bright lights and a large arsenal of weapons. Some of them were security guards at the temple, so Jesus asked: Why didn't you arrest me there, when I was with you teaching out in the open? They grabbed him. He didn't resist arrest. His friends tried to fight for him, but he stopped them, saying that violence only causes more violence. They ran away and abandoned him, leaving him alone with the police.

Jesus, how should I respond to hate?

The biggest surprise in Blanchard's "gay vision" is what is missing. He doesn't show history's most famous same-sex kiss, the kiss of betrayal between Judas and Jesus. Blanchard also ignores a subplot that fascinates many queer Bible scholars: the naked young man who ran away from the arrest in Mark 14:51. Several books have been written debating the authenticity and meaning of the Secret Gospel of Mark, which tells how the young man "learned the mysteries of God" by spending a night naked with Jesus.

Kissing was a common form of greeting in Biblical times, but Judas' treacherous man-on-man kiss has been a vehicle to instill homophobia for centuries, equating homosexuality with sin against God. It was a particularly intimate form of betrayal, prompting Jesus to ask, "Judas, would you betray me with a kiss?" Artists have been depicting the Judas kiss ever since the earliest known cycle on the life of Christ: the sixth-century mosaics of Ravenna, Italy. Since then artists have included the Judas kiss in almost every arrest scene, often with violence and chaos erupting around the couple. Blanchard must have figured that people have seen it way too often... although the Judas kiss remains a popular subject for most LGBT artists and viewers. In the 2009 *Circus Christi* series, Spanish artist Fernando Bayona Gonzalez changes it into a common contemporary crime: A kiss between gay lovers provokes a deadly gay bashing.

Blanchard keeps the focus firmly on the arrest of Jesus. His painting raises the specter of police harassment for homosexuality. Before the 1960s police in the United States routinely made surprise visits to gay bars, where mortified customers submitted willingly to arrest. Then sparks of open resistance began to transform the raids into rallies for gay rights. Police raids on two Los Angeles gay bars, the Black Cat Tavern in 1967 and the Patch in 1968, led to protest demonstrations and the creation of two major organizations for the LGBT community: Metropolitan Community Churches and the Advocate magazine.

In New York City the Stonewall Inn catered to the poorest and most marginalized queer people: drag queens, transgender folk, male prostitutes, and homeless gay youth. Their rebellion against a police raid in June 1969 became known as the start of the modern LGBT rights movement. They dared to stand up against an unjust system. Although they were not saints in the ordinary sense, they performed the miracle of transforming self-hatred into pride. Their courage galvanized a community and inspired an equality movement that is still growing stronger after more than four decades. The Stonewall uprising is commemorated around the world during June as LGBT Pride Month. When Jesus was arrested, he told his friends not to fight violence with violence, and they abandoned him. The lasting legacy of Stonewall comes from those people who neither ran away nor responded in kind. Instead they met violence with creative solutions and a commitment to a society where oppression is replaced by love. ●

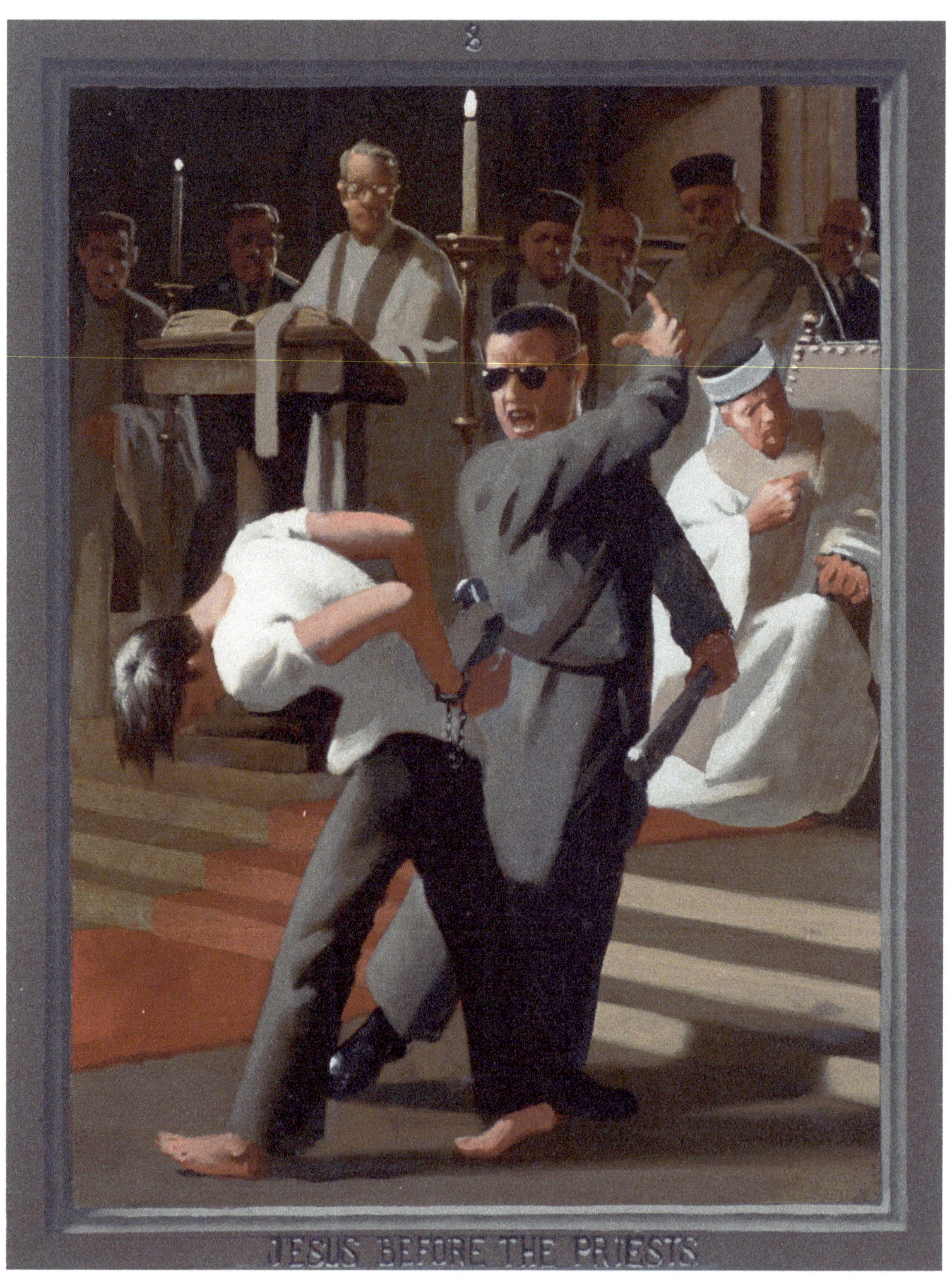

COLLECTION OF THE ARTIST

8. Jesus Before the Priests

"One of the officers standing by struck Jesus with his hand, saying, 'Is that how you answer the high priest?'" —John 18:22

A guard hits Jesus in a house of worship while clergymen do nothing, indifferent to the violence in *Jesus Before the Priests*. The blow is so hard that Jesus doubles over. The guard's dark sunglasses cannot hide his hateful grimace. A bespectacled priest looks up from an open Bible, but his bland face registers no concern for Jesus. Another cleric deliberately ignores the assault, studying his fingernails. Red carpet on the steps leads to an altar with candles. Watching from the back are more white-robed priests and men in business suits.

This is one of the more shocking images in Blanchard's Passion series because it exposes blatant religious hypocrisy in a benign contemporary setting. The church and its ministers look familiar, maybe even comforting or boring. One might expect violence from police or soldiers on the streets, but not in an ordinary church sanctuary with approval from the priests. In the banality of evil, unspeakable acts are committed not by monsters, but by regular people who accept the premises of an institution and follow orders.

Jesus Before the Priests is based on the Biblical story of Jesus' trial before Caiaphas, the high priest in the Jewish court of the Sanhedrin. After his arrest Jesus was judged first by the religious leaders of his own people. He threatened their power structures by following a God who was not confined to dogmatic boxes or controlled by religious institutions. The priests hurriedly called an emergency session of the Sanhedrin in the dead of night. The specific charge against Jesus was blasphemy. False witnesses were brought in to accuse him, but their testimony was inconsistent. During hours of questioning, Jesus mostly kept quiet, giving only a few cryptic answers. Finally they declared him guilty. Then the priests spat in his face and beat him before hustling him off to the Roman authorities for sentencing.

The Sanhedrin trial has never been an especially popular subject in art history, but Blanchard finds the inherent drama in the scene by approaching it from a contemporary gay viewpoint. LGBT people often come into conflict with churches because of who they love. When viewed with queer eyes, this painting is a painful reminder that it feels like a slap in the face to be told that God condemns homosexuality or "hates the sin but loves the sinner." LGBT people have been attacked with "clobber passages" from the Bible or tortured in "pray the gay away" therapy, also known as reparative or ex-gay conversion therapy. While today's LGBT artists mostly ignore the trial of Jesus, several have exposed the ancient purity laws that threaten queer people. For example, Swedish artist Elisabeth Ohlson Wallin photographed local LGBT people in Jerusalem with the offensive scriptures projected on or near their bodies in her 2010 *Jerusalem* series.

Conservative Christians cherry-pick Bible verses from Leviticus to condemn homosexuality on religious grounds, but these rules do not necessarily apply today. The passages refer specifically to sex with male temple prostitutes in the fertility cults of the neighboring Canaanite nations. They were only intended to stop ancient Jews from adopting the idolatrous practices of other cultures, not as a blanket prohibition on same-sex relationships forever. Anyway, Christians need not try to enforce laws from Leviticus. The New Testament firmly rejects imposing the old purity code on new Gentile Christian converts because Jesus replaced the old laws with the new commandment to love. Many of the other laws in Leviticus were abandoned by Christians long ago. In addition to its sexual rules, Leviticus also outlaws tattoos, eating shrimp, reading horoscopes, and wearing blended fabrics. Progressive Jews also find ways to disagree with these passages by taking them seriously but not literally.

Religions have often labeled queers as "sinners" and then refused to accept responsibility for the resulting violence. A 21st-century example occurred in Uganda, where a law that imposed the death penalty for homosexuality was drafted under the influence of Christian conservatives from America. Church trials for homosexuality continue in America too. Priests, ministers, and congregations are still being found guilty and rebuked, ousted, expelled, shunned, or silenced for such "crimes" as speaking in favor of LGBT rights, performing same-sex marriages, or ordaining LGBT clergy. Queer Christian art has been denounced as blasphemy, the same crime for which Jesus was condemned to death.

The ugly pattern is repeated with other groups. The Bible teaches love, but it has been used to justify slavery, wife-beating, genocide, and other horrors. *Jesus Before the Priests* sums up all religious hypocrisy in a single image. Religion, which supposedly promotes peace, justice, and love, instead has often become the impetus for war, discrimination, and acts of hate. Christians claim to follow Jesus, but if he showed up today they might reject him as a heretic and a troublemaker, just as the priests did 2,000 years ago. ●

"The Human One must undergo great suffering, and be **rejected** by the elders and chief priests...." —Luke 9:22*

The police arrested Jesus and took him straight to the priests—the ones whom Jesus had often accused of hypocrisy. These priests rigorously enforced minor rules, while neglecting the purpose of God's law: love and justice. They were like today's church officials who put ministers on trial for blessing same-sex relationships or ordaining lesbians and gays. The priests interrogated Jesus for hours, trying to get him to say something that could be used against him. When they asked about his teachings, Jesus replied, Why ask me? Ask those who heard me. At that, an officer struck him, snarling, Is that how you answer the high priest?! The priests watched the violence with bland indifference. There were some good men among them, but they accepted their role as part of the system. They kept silent as evil triumphed. Violence in God's name was routine. The unthinkable had become normal.

Jesus, I follow your example, even if it goes against what the church leaders say.

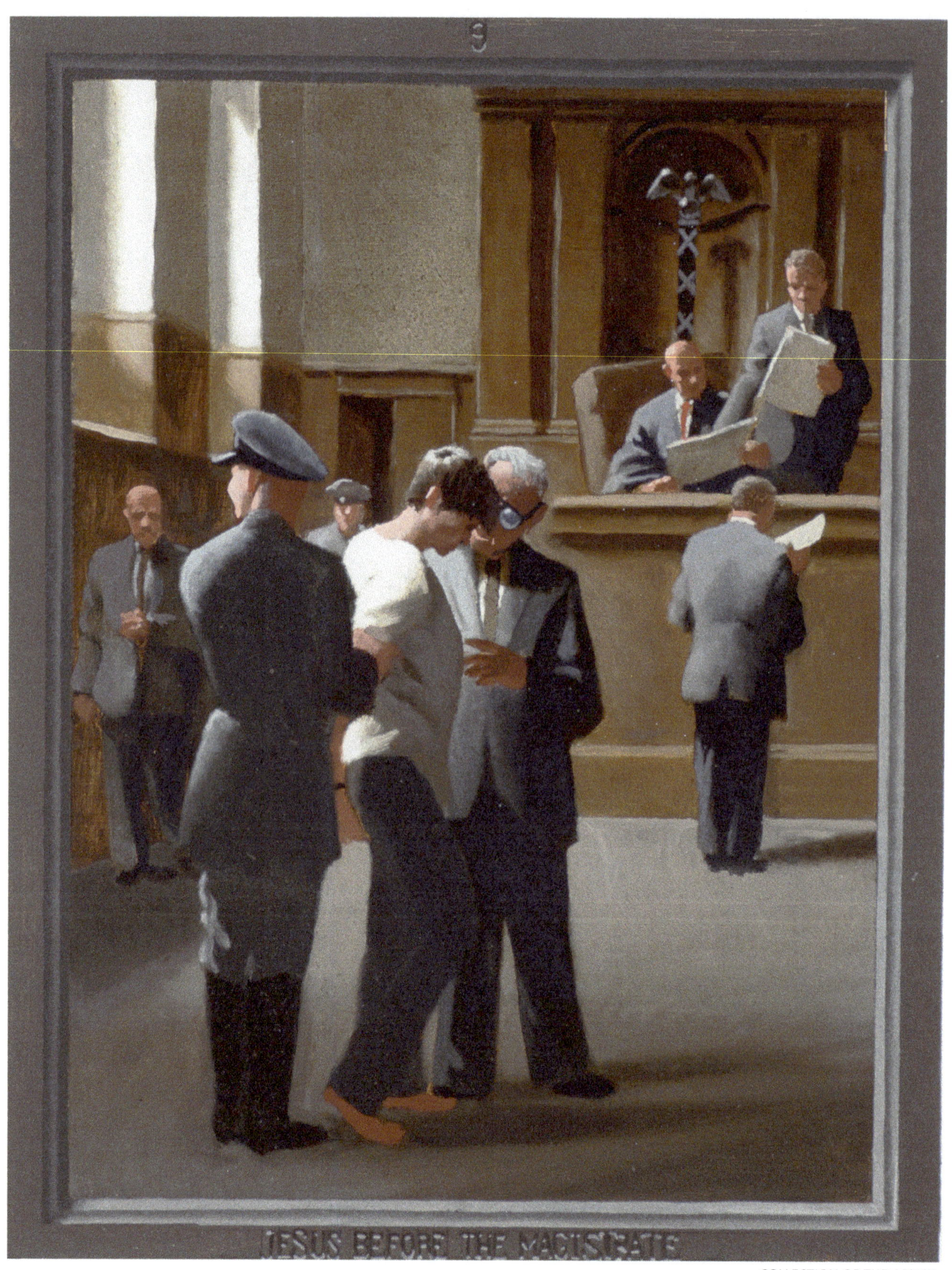

COLLECTION OF THE ARTIST

9. Jesus Before the Magistrate

"But he gave him no answer, not even to a single charge; so that the governor wondered greatly." —Matthew 27:14

A defendant refuses to accept a plea bargain in *Jesus Before the Magistrate*. Jesus is caught between his lawyer and a guard wearing knee-high military jackboots. Dull men in suits are shuffling papers, but nothing seems to happen in the generic courtroom. All of them, even the judge, look like faceless pawns in a menacingly complex bureaucracy. There is no jury. A pole behind the judge's bench is topped by an eagle, a symbol shared by imperial Rome—and the United States. In this antiseptic setting, impartial to a fault, Jesus is found guilty of treason and sentenced to death.

This painting is a modern version of Jesus' trial before the Roman governor, Pontius Pilate. The Bible says that after the priests found Jesus guilty, they took him to the governor for a second trial. Jesus was a Jew convicted of blasphemy under the laws of his own people, but this was no crime in the eyes of the Roman occupation forces. The priests wanted Jesus executed, so they switched the charge to treason, a capital offense under the law of the Roman government that occupied their land. The Bible is packed with juicy dialogue, characters, and details about the interrogation and interactions between Jesus and Pilate. The episode has been dramatized—and sometimes over-dramatized—as the first stop in the traditional Stations of the Cross. The sensational scene has been a crowd-pleaser in medieval Passion plays and contemporary films about the life of Christ. In all four gospel accounts Pilate tries various tactics to avoid responsibility for killing Jesus. The angry mob and the seriousness of the charges eventually force Pilate to authorize the death penalty. The Roman and Jewish leaders were enemies, but they put aside their dif-

"And **they began to accuse him,** saying,

'We found this man perverting our nation.'" —Luke 23:2

The priests took Jesus to the magistrate, Pontius Pilate, demanding that he impose the death penalty. His government headquarters was bustling with dispassionate bureaucrats. For Jesus, the only law was love—outright love for God and for neighbor. He kept quiet in this alien place where loveless laws led to injustice. They used the legal system to force an uneasy "peace" on the local people, suppressing their culture and their very identity. Pilate's lawmakers were like those who devised the "don't ask, don't tell" policy or "defense of marriage act." Pilate came from just such a narrow-minded viewpoint when he asked Jesus, What have you done? Jesus answered, I have come into the world to bear witness to the truth. Puzzled, the magistrate posed another question: What is truth?

Jesus, show me your truth.

ferences to kill the man who loved without limits.

Jesus' trial before Pilate is one of the most enduring images in Christian art, dating back to fourth-century sarcophagi in the Catacombs of Rome. Some artists portray Pilate as a harsh tyrant or a clever politician, but Blanchard opts to show him as an uncaring bureaucrat, too bland to make a memorable villain. This painting takes the whole overblown scenario and strips away the embellishments that have been cultivated by countless artists over the centuries: There are no priests accusing Jesus of "perverting" the nation. Jesus does not engage in one-on-one repartee with the governor. King Herod, Barabbas, and Pilate's wife never appear. Pilate does not ritually wash his hands to absolve himself. Blanchard condenses all the action into a single, simple scene. The understated result is one of the most tranquil images in his whole Passion series. The painting gets at the unvarnished truth: Jesus was a nobody in the Roman justice system. The decision to kill the child of God was no big deal. It happened without fanfare, and it could happen again now somewhere closer to home. Ultimately Jesus was executed for treason, but his "crime" might have gone by a different name in another time and place.

Queer people can relate to the experience of being trapped in a system that is rigged against them. The deadly pattern of oppression begins with words of insult that serve to demonize and dehumanize a target group, paving the way for acts of violence. This hard truth is illustrated in *Stations of the Cross: The Struggle For LGBT Equality,* a series of 15 paintings completed in 2013 by Tennessee artist Mary Button. In the first station she juxtaposes Jesus being condemned to death with the first use of the gay insult "faggot" in print (in a 1913 guide to criminal slang). Name-calling can escalate to assault. Anti-gay slurs are part of the continuum of oppression that includes murder by those who aim to purge society of sexual minorities. Even where there is no state-sponsored persecution, people must fight to pass laws that recognize same-sex unions and protect LGBT people from discrimination. The courtroom scene of the gay Passion could happen again now in a world where many countries still outlaw same-sex acts between consenting adults. A handful of nations still punish them with death. ●

The courtroom scene of the gay Passion could happen again now.

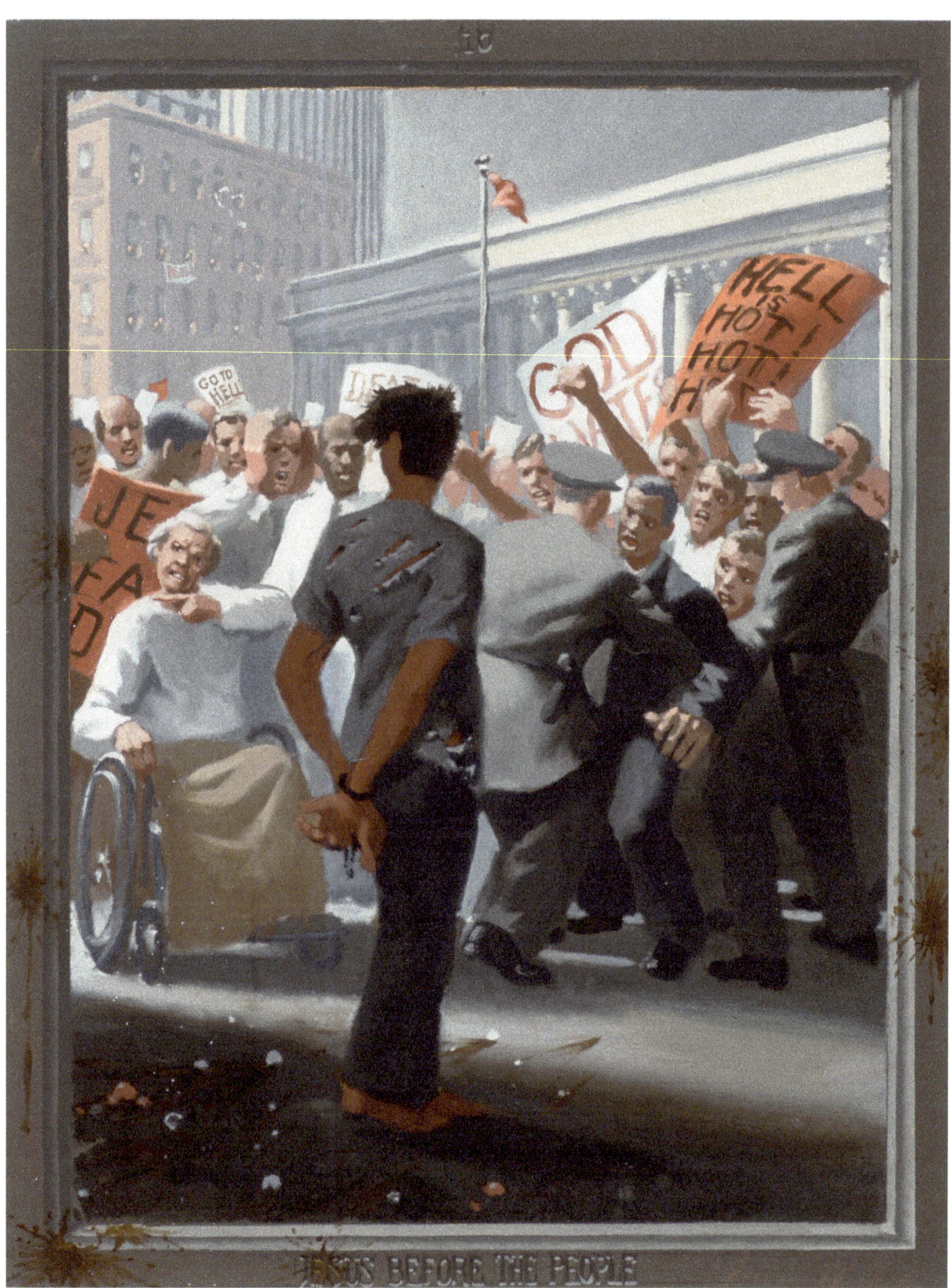

PRIVATE COLLECTION

10. Jesus Before the People

"Behold the man!" —John 19:5

An angry mob confronts a young prisoner in *Jesus Before the People*. Jesus stands alone, handcuffed and motionless in the shadows, before the religious zealots picketing outside the courthouse. He twists his body, turning the other cheek to the crowd that assaults him with insults and rotten eggs. They are enraged, shouting, shaking fists, and waving signs with messages such as "God hates..." The last word is hidden, so the viewer can fill in the blank. This lynch mob could be turning against any disadvantaged group. His head is haloed by a sign demanding "Death to...." Another sign warns, "Hell is hot, hot, hot!" Someone adds an obscene gesture by flipping the finger at Jesus.

A man in a wheelchair points his index finger sideways, signaling to cut his throat or get the hell out. Police struggle to stop the hostile crowd from killing Jesus right there. He turns his back on the viewer, revealing slashes in his tattered T-shirt. Eggshells, squashed tomatoes, and other debris litter the ground after being hurled at Jesus. Even the frame looks like it is spattered with eggs and gunk in a trompe l'oeil (fool the eye) artistic technique. The only barrier between the mob and the viewer is Jesus.

The words on the signs suggest that Jesus is a gay man being jeered by fundamentalists. These look like the "God hates fags" signs carried by hate-mongers from Westboro Baptist Church at AIDS funerals and pride marches. *Jesus Before the People* shows the plight of any individual pressured by a group. By scapegoating vulnerable people, bullies maintain power. Blanchard doesn't dehumanize the demonstrators or resort to demeaning stereotypes. The crowd is multi-racial, but all male, which is realistic for mass street violence.

This painting updates the Biblical episode where Jesus was paraded before the bloodthirsty mob after being whipped. Pilate, the

Roman governor, displayed the beaten Jesus to the crowd, exclaiming, "Behold the man!" They responded by shouting, "Crucify him!" The scene is all the more tragic because the crowds adored Jesus less than a week earlier when he entered the city. But the enemies of Jesus managed to stir up enough hate to turn the public against their former hero. In all four gospels Pilate yields to the crowd. He reluctantly sentences Jesus to death, trying to escape responsibility by blaming it on the people. In Matthew's gospel he literally washes his hands in a public ritual to cleanse himself of guilt. Later interpreters have seen the sympathetic portrayal of Pilate as an attempt to cover up the role of the Roman government in Jesus' death. The scene has been used to fuel anti-Semitism as Jews were scapegoated as "Christ-killers," despite the fact that Jesus himself was a Jew, as were his apostles. The crowd in Jerusalem was lashing out at one of their own, erupting in the horizontal violence that often happens among oppressed people, including the LGBT community.

Numerous artists have painted the scene, which is known to art historians by the Latin phrase *Ecce Homo* (usually translated as "Behold the man"). Like many images from the Passion, the Ecce Homo theme first appeared in art around the 10th century. It was re-enacted in the Passion plays of medieval theater and became popular in the Renaissance, depicted not only in Passion cycles but also on altarpieces and in sculpture groups. Most versions followed the same pattern, showing Jesus, Pilate, and the unruly crowd in a Jerusalem cityscape. Artists occasionally included self-portraits, inserting themselves into history either as Christ or as a member of the crowd. Dutch Early Renaissance painter Hieronymus Bosch wreaked revenge on the anti-Jesus mob by turning their faces into ugly caricatures. During the late Renaissance, artists began to show Jesus alone in the Ecce Homo episode. They created a new subject called Man of Sorrows: a close-up of the anguished face and upper body of Jesus as he was presented to his detractors. Blanchard's version takes the iconography in the opposite direction, expanding the crowd and turning Jesus away from the viewer.

Modern artists have adapted the Ecce Homo theme to convey other forms of human suffering and degradation. German Expressionists seemed to have a special affinity for the motif. Otto Dix illustrated the brutality of war in *Ecce Homo with Self Likeness Behind Barbed Wire*. George Grosz satirized human greed, lust, and cruelty with his *Ecce Homo* collection of vignettes from 1920s Berlin. In contemporary times the Latin word *homo* naturally lends itself to LGBT interpretations. Swedish photographer Elisabeth Ohlson Wallin used it as the name for her famous 1998 photo series recreating the life of Christ with LGBT models. Ecce Homo became a pun meaning both "Behold the man" and "Behold the homosexual." ●

"They shouted out, 'Crucify, crucify him!'" —Luke 23:21

How quickly the people turned against Jesus! Less than a week ago the crowds adored him. Now a mob was outside the government headquarters demanding his death. Pilate, who ruled as governor and magistrate, wanted above all to maintain security. He made Jesus stand before the angry throng. They shouted with increasing frenzy: "Crucify him!" The chief priests stirred up the crowd, vehemently accusing Jesus of all kinds of sins. "He's a traitor! Burn in hell!" Their words still echo today when hate-mongers tell ruthless lies: "God hates gays! Death to fags!" The magistrate saw that a riot was beginning. If one person had to die to keep the peace, then the end justified the means. Guilt or innocence was not part of the equation. The magistrate agreed to the demands of the crowd. He ordered the execution of Jesus.

Jesus, have I let others pressure me into doing something wrong?

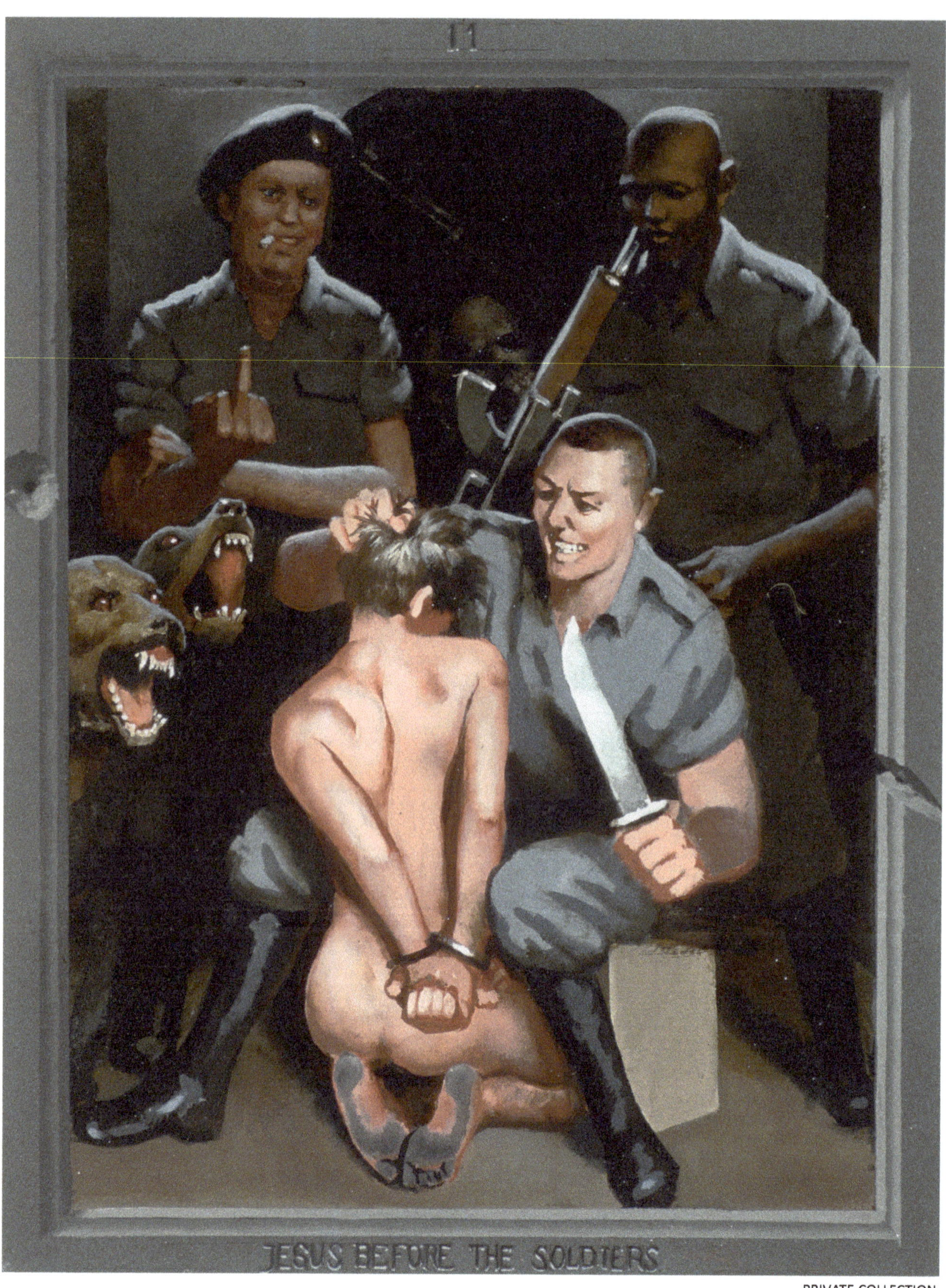

PRIVATE COLLECTION

11. Jesus Before the Soldiers

"Soldiers treated him with contempt and mocked him." —Luke 23:11

Marine look-alikes torment a naked prisoner in *Jesus Before the Soldiers*. Jesus kneels, naked and vulnerable, as a knife-wielding soldier grabs him by the hair. War dogs bark at him like hounds of hell, baring their teeth. A leering soldier flips the finger at him while another brandishes an assault rifle. Behind them a skull stares out from a gaping black hole. A dark halo seems to arch over him. The soft, round curves of Jesus' exposed buttocks make the blade of the knife look even sharper. Dust clings to the soles of Jesus' bare feet. Even the frame bears the scars of war: a bullet hole and a gash.

The soldiers smirk, compelling viewers to laugh with them as they hurt and humiliate their victim. And yet the torturers still look human, perhaps even handsome. The viewer is pushed to become an accomplice, unable to change the course of events. The only choice is to turn the page, closing one's eyes on human suffering, or to watch and perhaps pray. The reason to relive the horror of what happened to Jesus is to bear witness to the ongoing suffering that the Passion represents. Perhaps it can motivate compassionate action in the present.

This picture begins a section of four explicitly violent images leading to the crucifixion. When considering Blanchard's paintings of violence and nudity, it is essential to keep them in the holy context of Christ's life. Such explosive subjects must be handled with care. Otherwise they may serve to glorify violence or fuel sadomasochistic fantasies, adding to the exploitation pictured. This painting and the next one (*Jesus is Beaten*) may well be the most terrifying images in Blanchard's Passion. They are the only paintings in the series to combine

"He was despised and rejected...

a man of sorrows, and acquainted with grief." —Isaiah 53:3

The soldiers stripped off Jesus' clothes and mocked him with contempt. They made ethnic jokes about him for being Jewish, and taunted him as a "king" because he taught that God's kingdom of love is here and now. They could have used "queer" or a "faggot" or "lezzy" or any other slur. Whatever the words, whenever one person insults another, a child of God is humiliated. The soldiers were young men similar to Jesus in many ways. The bullying was done by the soldiers, but the religious leaders were also to blame for the cruelty. The priests had set the stage for violence by calling Jesus a sinner. They targeted Jesus, but the pain spread far beyond him to terrorize many more people.

Jesus, what can I do to bring peace?

violence and nudity. It hurts to look at them. After these, death comes as a relief. Maybe that's the point. In these two images the frames are especially important because they keep the naked torture in context. All 24 images in the series have inseparable frames specifying their title and their number in the series. Blanchard painted the frames directly on the same wooden panel with each image, ensuring that the suffering will be seen as part of a larger story. His Passion paintings report the truth about violence. At the same time he condenses the barrage of brutality into a few images suitable for deeper reflection.

Jesus Before the Soldiers is the modern equivalent of Jesus being mocked by Roman soldiers in gospel accounts. They stripped him and dressed him up as a king with a crown of thorns and a reed for a scepter. Then they ridiculed him by bowing down with pretend praise: "Hail, king of the Jews." As still happens today, verbal abuse was a warm-up for serious physical assault. They spat on him and beat him on the head with the reed.

Graphic violence was not depicted in Christianity's first millennium, but since the 10th century grisly depictions of the Passion have been used to condone war and other forms of violence. Evidence suggests that early Christian artists cared more about how Christ's spirit lived on in them than about how he died. Christianity was also relatively tolerant of homosexuality for a thousand years after Jesus died. Then the 10th and 11th centuries brought the first Crusades, the first gruesome artistic depictions of Jesus suffering on the cross, and the first church council saying that homosexuals should be burned at the stake. Atonement theologies arose saying that God wanted Jesus to suffer on the cross to pay the price or "atone" for human sin. Church leaders started encouraging believers to meditate on how Jesus was punished for their own individual sins. Blanchard's Passion questions, dismantles, and frees people from that deadly mindset through a gay vision of God suffering with humanity in the Passion.

With this painting Blanchard employs an unusual composition in which Jesus is seen from behind. The viewer can't see the face of Jesus. In art history the mocking of Christ is traditionally shown with Jesus blindfolded and facing the viewer. One of the most popular versions is an unfinished painting by Fra Angelico, an early Italian Renaissance artist and friar. His idealized Christ remains at peace even when slapped by disembodied hands. Blanchard's interpretation has more in common with the modern, humanistic view in *Jesus Mocked by the Soldiers* by avant-garde French painter Edouard Manet. When it was first exhibited in 1860, critics reviled Manet for vulgarity because he used lower-class models and pictured the near-naked Jesus as an ordinary man.

Blanchard has acknowledged that one of the artists who influenced his view of the Passion is modern American painter Leon Golub. He was a figurative expressionist who painted scenes of military and paramilitary torture in his 1980s series *Mercenaries, Interrogations,* and *White Squads.* Blanchard echoes Golub's compositions and moral tone, mixing political critique with artistic sensibility. Today's artists almost never paint LGBT versions of Jesus being mocked. Instead they get accused of mocking Jesus whenever they portray him as queer.

Blanchard's version of soldiers mocking Christ owes its imagery not only to masterpieces of art, but also to shocking photos that dominated the news during his painting process. This panel and the next were both completed in 2004, the same year the news media revealed snapshots of American soldiers and military contractors torturing Iraqi prisoners at Abu Ghraib prison in Baghdad. The abuse occurred during a war sparked by the 9/11 terrorist attacks on the World Trade Center. Blanchard is a New Yorker who painted the Passion while in turmoil over the attacks that led to the war. Here he addresses the potent connection between religion, terrorism, and torture.

The painting makes a visual protest against all forms of bullying and torture, including "ex-gay conversion therapy" that aims to change the sexual orientation of LGBT people. Thousands have been subjected to harmful techniques such as pairing homosexual imagery with electric shocks or nausea-inducing medication. The trauma endured by Blanchard's contemporary Christ is not an isolated incident, but a theme that recurs in human history and perhaps the human heart. With this image, all victims become one with Christ and receive a chance for compassionate attention from the viewer. ●

The painting makes a visual protest against all forms of bullying and torture.

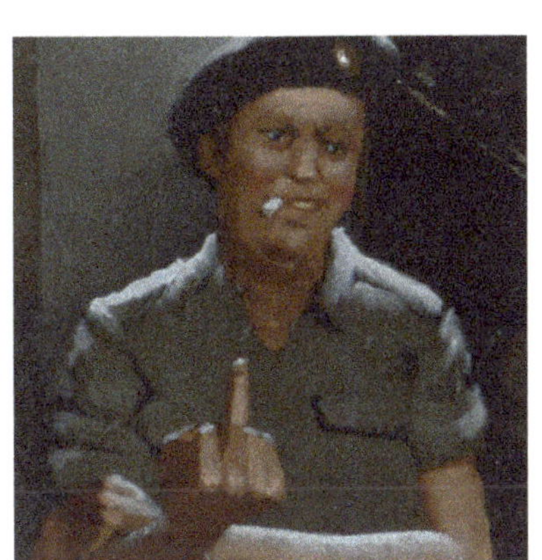

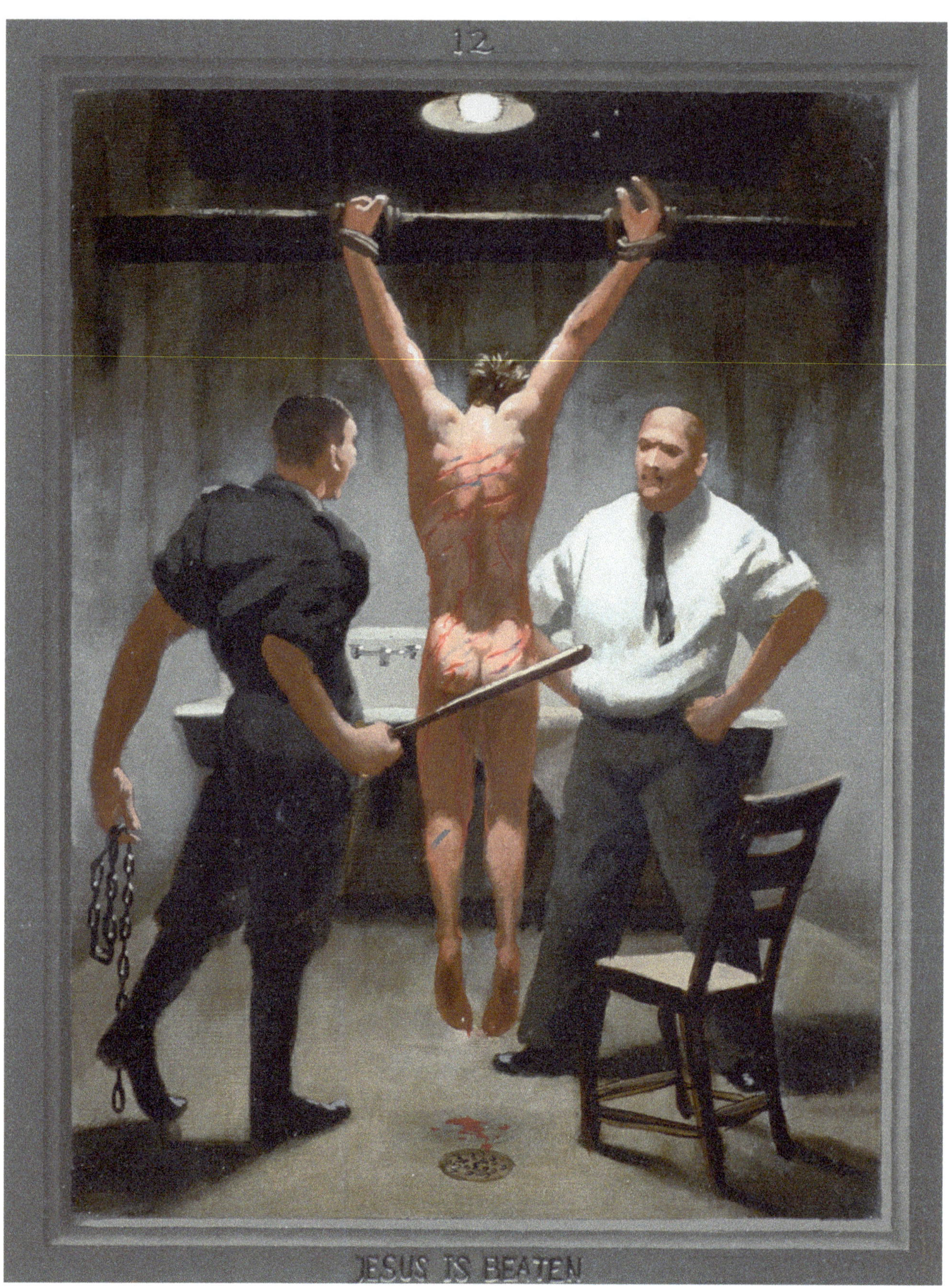

COLLECTION OF THE ARTIST

12. Jesus is Beaten

"Then Pilate took Jesus and scourged him." —John 19:1

A naked prisoner hangs helpless while a soldier hits him with a club and chain in *Jesus is Beaten*. His precious blood drips into a drain in the floor. A man in a necktie supervises with grim determination. The torture occurs in a bleak, gray room. It is bare except for a sink and an empty chair. The anonymous victim is turned away from the viewer, so only his wounded backside is visible. He cannot be identified as Jesus except by reading his name in the title on the frame. A ceiling lamp forms a distant halo over the head of the battered Jesus, casting shadows in the starkly lit torture chamber.

Jesus is Beaten is perhaps the most disturbing of the 24 paintings in Blanchard's Passion. Blood is shed here for the first time in the series. The nudity stirs up sexual tension and an almost unbearable sense of vulnerability. It is similar to the previous image (*Jesus Before the Soldiers*) as a scene of violence inflicted on a naked man. There is no other nudity in the rest of series. Despite the sadomasochistic undertones, Blanchard refused to allow the scene to be taken out of its holy context. He painted the frame and title directly on the wooden panel, redeeming the horror by establishing it as an integral event in the life of Jesus.

The scourging of Jesus is mentioned briefly in gospel accounts and was standard procedure before crucifixion under Roman law. *Jesus is Beaten* is a new interpretation of Jesus being scourged, a scene often called "The Flagellation" in art history. Crucifixion scenes dominate Christianity today, but early Christians emphasized the risen Christ, depicting his life instead of his suffering and death. Images of Jesus being whipped first began to appear in art around the 10th century, along with other increasingly gruesome scenes from the Passion. During this period the church also began to encourage self-flagellation as a way for believers to share in the suffering of Christ.

Artists usually depict the Flagellation by showing Jesus with two men who flog him. After the 12th century Jesus almost always faces the viewer while he is whipped, but Blanchard reverts to an earlier tradition by showing him from behind. A well-known version was painted by Italian Renaissance painter Piero della Francesca, who places the scourging in a pristine tiled courtyard with perfect perspective. There is a homoerotic flavor to many of these historic paintings of the Flagellation, including the robust versions by Caravaggio and Rubens. The same-sex sadomasochism was made explicit in the 1990s by gay artist Delmas Howe. His *Stations: A Gay Passion* includes an erotic flagellation scene with near-naked men in leather fetish gear at the gay sex piers of New York City in the 1970s.

Like the previous panel, *Jesus is Beaten* is reminiscent of the Abu Ghraib prisoner abuse photos that became public when Blanchard was painting these images. It delivers a shocking glimpse of the trauma that is inflicted behind closed doors. Apart from the frame, there is no way to identify the prisoner in this painting as Jesus—except by remembering his words, "Whatever you do to the least of these, you do to me." ●

It delivers a shocking glimpse of the trauma that is inflicted behind closed doors.

"Do not weep for me, but **weep for yourselves**
and for your children." —Luke 23:28

Pilate, the Roman governor, ordered that Jesus be scourged—a severe whipping before execution. This cruel punishment was state-sponsored terrorism against a man who defied the established order and hierarchy by teaching unlimited love for all. When they hit him, they did violence to everyone who has ever dared to be different. We are the body of Christ, and every individual's suffering affects the whole. The charge against Jesus was treason, but his "crime" might have gone by a different name in another time and place. Governments and churches have imposed similar tortures on people who don't fit in or threaten the system in various ways, including homosexuality. Those who carry out the dreadful orders are demeaned in the process too. The painful scourging left Jesus bleeding and in shock.

Jesus, be with all who suffer
... and with all who cause suffering.

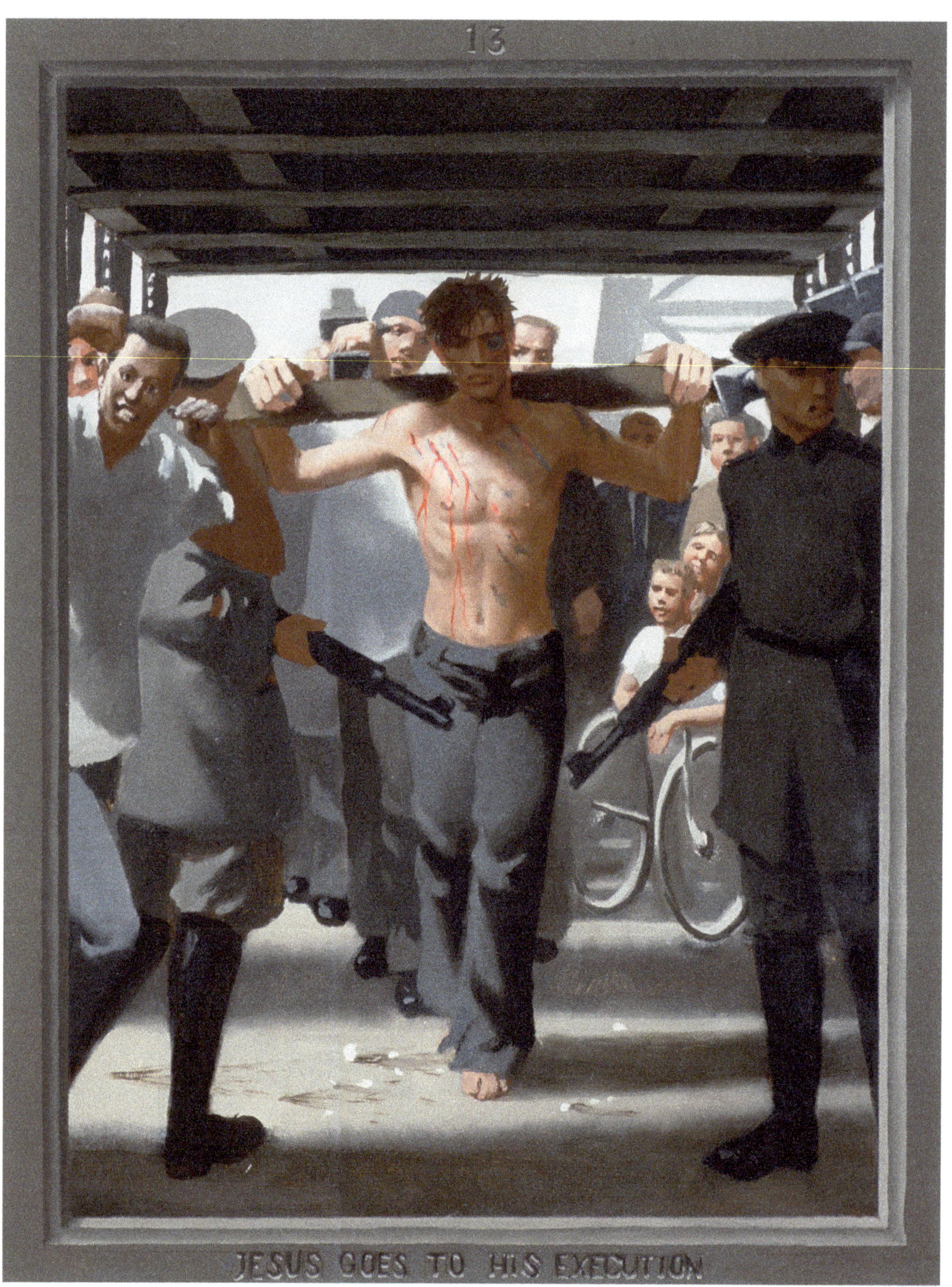

COLLECTION OF THE ARTIST

13. Jesus Goes to His Execution

"He went out, bearing his own cross, to the place called the place of a skull, which is called in Hebrew Golgotha." —John 19:17

A bloody prisoner carries a crossbeam through the city in *Jesus Goes to His Execution*. Jesus is surrounded by gun-toting guards. News reporters aim multiple cameras at him in a peculiarly contemporary form of intrusion. They broadcast his private pain to the world. He is walking barefoot to the execution site, carrying the means of his own death, the cross on which he will be crucified. He seems to bear the weight of the world on his shoulders. Nobody offers sympathy. A cheering spectator on the left looks out at the viewer, assuming that everyone shares his glee at seeing the blasphemer punished. A boy in a wheelchair watches with excitement, and perhaps relief that he is not being targeted this time. Jesus strides straight at the viewer with his face in shadow. His bare feet crunch the broken shells of eggs that were thrown at him. He seems to be walking under scaffolding on a construction site. The low, overhanging roof adds to the tension, loading the scene with a heavy sense of impending doom. Soon the viewer must move out of the way or get trampled.

All four gospels report that Jesus was forced to walk through Jerusalem to the execution grounds outside the city walls. Crucifixions were done on a hill resembling a skull. Thus it was named Golgotha (or Calvary in Latin), which means Place of the Skull. The Bible records two encounters along the way: A passerby named Simon, from the Libyan town of Cyrene, was enlisted to carry the cross for Jesus. And the women of Jerusalem followed him, wailing in grief. Knowing that the tragedy was much greater than his own personal suffering, Jesus turned to them and said, "Do not weep for me, but weep for yourselves and for your children." (Luke 23:28) In Blanchard's

"Surely he has borne our griefs and carried our sorrows." —Isaiah 53:4

The soldiers made Jesus walk to the execution grounds. They forced him to carry the cross on which he would be crucified. It was big news and crowds gathered along the road. They had watched Jesus rise to mass popularity, and now they wanted to see him fall. Many jeered at him. Some of the hecklers used to be his followers. Maybe they shouted louder than the rest to prove that they were not associated with Jesus—like closeted lawmakers who loudly oppose LGBT rights. For those whom God created queer, the struggle to be fully human in a homophobic world can be a heavy cross to bear.

Jesus, I will pull my own weight and walk with you.

version, Jesus is isolated in the center of the crowd. Nobody sympathizes or shares his burden.

Early Christians did not depict Christ suffering on the cross, but they did show him carrying it. Carrying the cross is one of the earliest and most enduring images in Christian art. The scene is sculpted in marble on a fourth-century sarcophagus from the Catacombs of Domitilla. In the early images the cross looks light and easy to carry, but over the centuries it got heavier until Jesus could barely drag it in late medieval art. From the start Jesus was usually shown in profile, almost never coming right at the viewer as in Blanchard's version.

Jesus carrying his cross is the heart of the traditional Stations of the Cross, a set of images that originated as stopping points for pilgrims along an actual road in Jerusalem. Known as the Via Dolorosa or Way of Sorrows, it is the route where the historical Jesus apparently walked to his execution. Eight of the traditional fourteen stations occur as Jesus carries his cross, falling three times under its tremendous weight and encountering various people. Blanchard crystallizes the eventful walk to Calvary into a single image. Until about 1100 artists most often showed the cross being carried by Simon of Cyrene, but then the burden shifted to Jesus. Artists also gradually increased the number of characters in the scene. The trend culminated in 1564 when Flemish artist Pieter Bruegel the Elder painted an enormous crowd of more than a hundred people accompanying Jesus through a vast landscape in *Procession to Calvary.*

Art history includes many variations on Jesus carrying his cross, including Renaissance masterpieces by Hieronymus Bosch, who caricatured the spectators with grotesque faces, and El Greco, whose haunting close-up showed an elongated Christ lifting his eyes to a stormy sky. Michelangelo bucked the trend by sculpting a muscular nude Jesus who practically swaggers with his cross. Modern mainstream artists have done surprisingly little with the motif of Jesus carrying his cross, preferring instead to draw inspiration from other scenes from Christ's Passion.

The road to Calvary has inspired some powerful LGBT Christian art. Swedish photographer Elisabeth Ohlson Wallin included it in her controversial *Ecce Homo* series that recreates the life of Christ in a contemporary LGBT context. In *Weighed Down by the Cross,* she shows Jesus stumbling under his cross through a crowd with red ribbons and a Names Project memorial panel, symbolizing AIDS as a Way of Sorrows. Tennessee artist Mary Button matches each traditional station with a milestone from the past 100 years of LGBT history in *Stations of the Cross: The Struggle For LGBT Equality.* She paints Jesus carrying his cross against a backdrop of violence aimed at queers, including Nazi persecution, the Stonewall Rebellion, and the assassination of gay politician Harvey Milk.

For LGBT people, their God-given sexuality may feel like a heavy load in a world that disapproves of being queer. Sometimes they learn to collaborate in their own oppression by carrying their own "cross" of internalized homophobia and self-hatred. Earlier in his life Jesus spoke of carrying the cross as a metaphor for the inevitable costs of the spiritual journey: "If any would come after me, let them deny themselves and take up their cross and follow me." (*Matthew 16:24) Many queer people must grapple with religion-based discrimination on their particular path to wholeness. ●

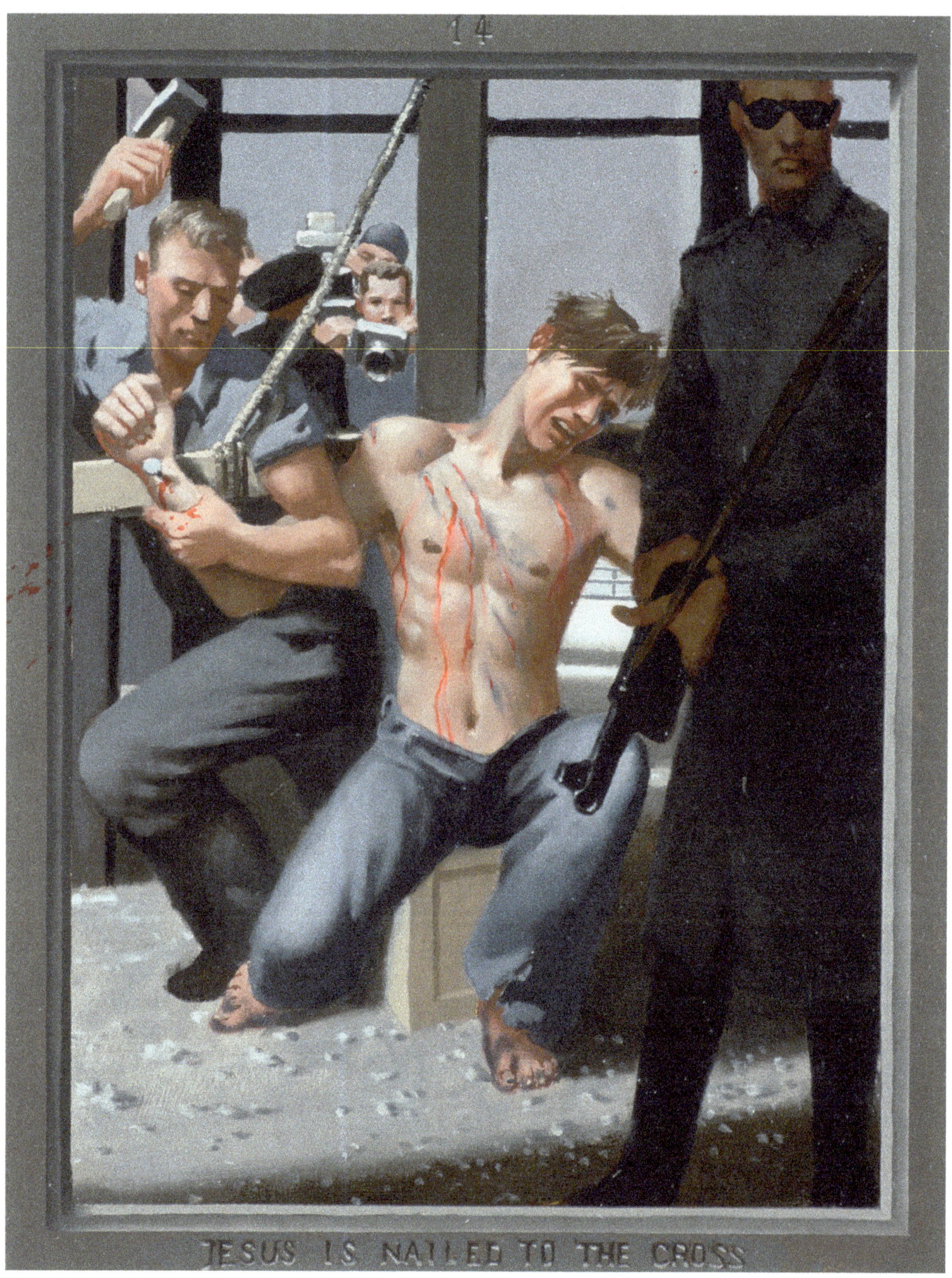

COLLECTION OF THE ARTIST

14. Jesus is Nailed to the Cross

"There they crucified him." —Luke 23:33

Bruised and bleeding, a condemned man cries out in agony as a spike is hammered through his wrist in *Jesus is Nailed to the Cross*. The guard shows no emotion as he pounds a cruel spike through human flesh and bone. A shadowy guard in sunglasses wields a rifle to keep spectators away. Paparazzi with cameras jockey for position, prying into the pain and making it a commodity for public consumption. A rope is ready to hoist Jesus up to the cross that looms in the background. Even the frame is splashed with blood.

Jesus grimaces. The pain is excruciating, a word that comes from the Latin *cruciare*, "to crucify." The viewer is right there, closer than the news cameras, close enough to get spattered with blood, to hear Jesus' cries and the metallic clank with every hammer blow. Of all 24 paintings in the series, this is the only one where the viewer can see distress on Jesus' face. Previously he was turned away or hidden in shadow when he felt pain. Now the viewer must look into his suffering face. This is also the bloodiest picture in the series. The painting forces the viewer to witness everything, to be an accomplice, voyeur, or victim. One of the beauties of this series is how even the men who torture and execute Jesus are still presented as real people. They are cruel or oblivious or blinded by the drive for power at any cost, but ultimately they remain human.

When the gospels were written, there was no need to explain what was meant by "they crucified him." The Bible doesn't describe it in detail. The terrors of the cross were all too familiar to first-century people. Blanchard actually spares the viewer some of the horror by skipping over other scenes reported in the gospels, such as Jesus being stripped, raised on the cross, and refusing the "benumbing drink" of wine mixed with gall.

At this point it may feel like overkill to show a blow-by-blow account of Jesus being crucified. But past artists, goaded by the Stations of the Cross format, often divided the crucifixion process into multiple steps. Compared to many historic paintings of this scene, Blanchard's Jesus looks active, like he might still be able to escape from the cross. Another painter who brings the horror of the crucifixion into a modern LGBT context is Mary Button. In her LGBT Stations of the Cross, Jesus is nailed to the cross while queer people are hooked to electrodes for electroshock therapy meant to "cure" homosexuality. In Blanchard's version a 21st-century gay man stands for everyone who has been victimized. The crucifixion of Jesus comes to symbolize all human suffering. ●

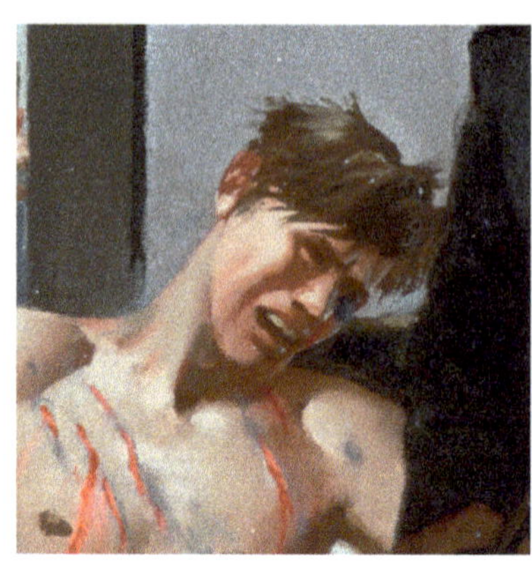

In Blanchard's vision a 21st-century gay man stands for everyone who has been victimized.

“They have pierced my hands and feet

—I can count all my bones—they stare and gloat over me.” —Psalm 22:16-17

The soldiers nailed Jesus to the cross. It was high noon on Friday. The pounding of the hammer left no room for neutrality. People were forced to choose sides, us versus them. If you didn't want to be a victim, you had to join the perpetrators. The psychic terror extended to those who watched. By abusing one person, the authorities intimidated everyone like him, everyone who was different in any way… religion, race, gender, sexual orientation, whatever. And what about the men who nailed him to the cross? Their actions were monstrous, but Jesus still saw their humanity. He prayed for the men who crucified him: God, forgive them because they don't know what they're doing.

God, help me find meaning in the brutal death of Jesus.

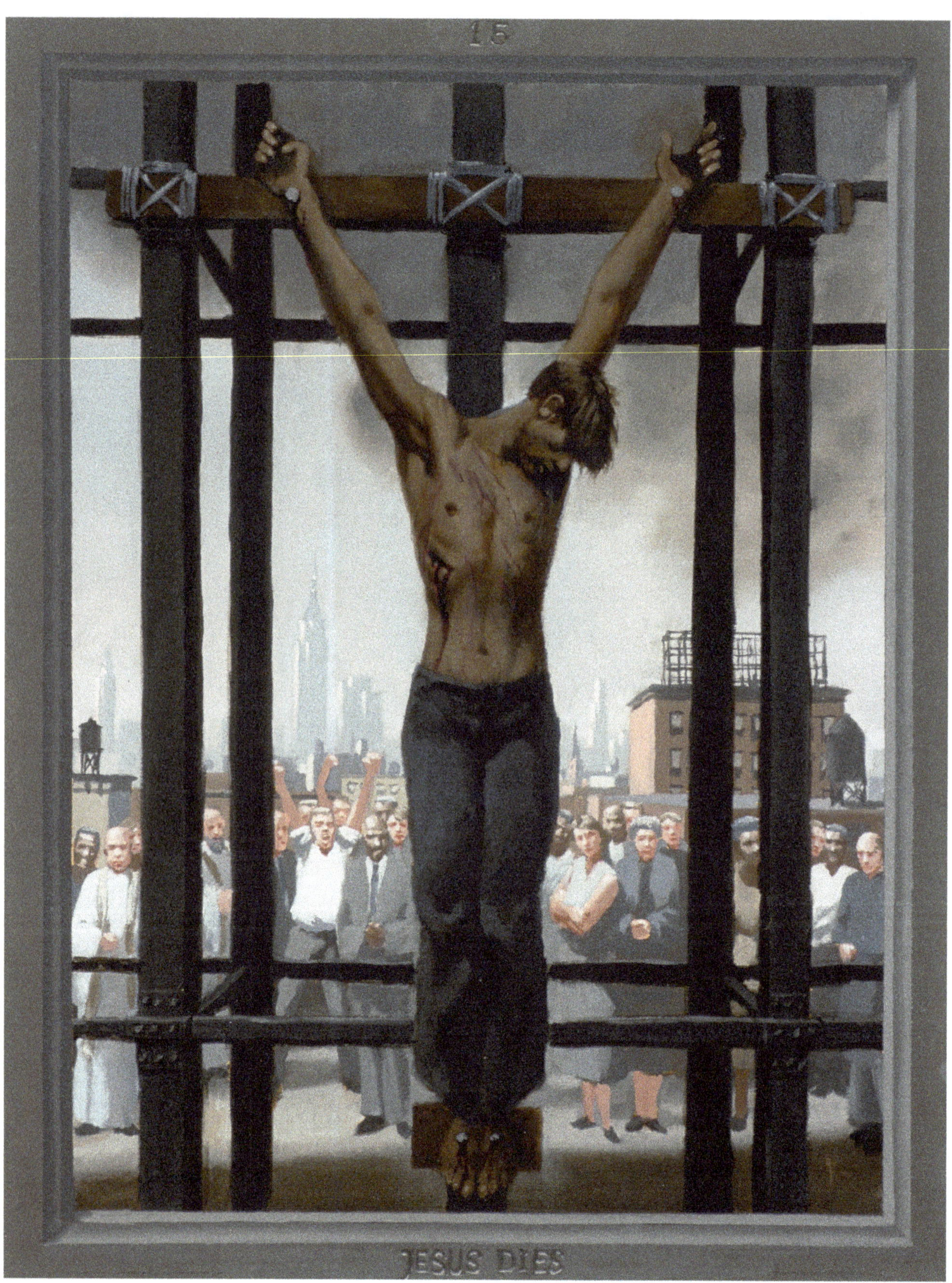

COLLECTION OF BRIAN LATHROP

15. Jesus Dies

"While the sun's light failed...he breathed his last." —Luke 23:45-46

Jesus Dies places the crucifixion of Christ against a modern city skyline. A young man hangs on scaffolding that forms a cross behind him. The body of Jesus looms large before the 21st-century crowd. Some jeer at the dying martyr while others pray. Many, including a few priests, watch grimly. Once again Jesus has brought together an unlikely group. These spectators look like ordinary people today. Jesus dies an outcast's death in pain and humiliation. He stayed true to his vision, even when it brought him into conflict with authorities, even to the point of death. Head bowed, Jesus looks like a corpse.

The crucifixion could be taking place on top of a building, or on some kind of terrace. The silhouette of a skyscraper like the Empire State Building stands tall in the distance. Its presence hints at a subtext of Blanchard's Passion: the 9/11 terrorist attacks happened near Blanchard's art studio while he was working on the series. The World Trade Center is missing from the skyline in this painting. It went up in smoke that hung over the city like the storm clouds that blot out the sun in the sky above Jesus.

Here the cross regains its uncomfortable power to disrupt lives. The crucifixion of Jesus is so important and widespread in Western culture that it is in danger of losing its impact from deadening over-repetition. Blanchard brings it back to life by updating the image, defying attempts to downplay the significance of the cross or turn it into an oversimplified test of faith. Even non-believers are moved by the story of the martyr who gave his life for others. For Christians it means that God loved people enough to become one of us. Some see the crucifixion as a sacrifice required by God

"He said, 'It is finished'; and he bowed his head and gave up his spirit." —John 19:30

Jesus knows the worst human suffering from his own personal experience. As he hung dying on the cross, a few of his supporters watched. Among them were his mother and the man he loved. After about three hours on the cross, Jesus shouted, My God, my God, why have you forsaken me? All the misery of a broken world seemed to come together at the crossroads of that awful moment. Nothing left, he emptied himself completely. The death of Jesus was unique, and yet it was also terribly common. His execution was one link in a long chain of human violence. Whenever anyone commits violence against another, Christ is crucified.

My God, don't you care?!
Why have you forsaken us?

to redeem the world from human sins. Others view it as God suffering with humanity, longing to stop the cycle of violence. The mystery of the cross is remembered by the faithful through the bread and cup of the Eucharist, the central sacrament of church life.

All four gospels provide detailed yet differing reports of what happened while Jesus hung on the cross. Darkness fell over the land for about three hours as the crowds mocked Jesus. He had a few short conversations. Speaking from the cross, Jesus entrusted his mother and his Beloved Disciple into each other's care. One of his last wishes was to make them into an unconventional family. He called to his mother, Woman, behold your son! And to his beloved, he said, Behold your mother! The unnamed "disciple whom Jesus loved" is referenced five times in the gospel of John (John 13:23, 19:26, 20:2, 21:7, 21:20). He reclined next to Jesus at the Last Supper, resting his head on Jesus' chest. He was the only male disciple present at the crucifixion. The scene was even included in the new Scriptural Stations of the Cross instituted by the Pope in 1991. The Scriptural Stations also flesh out the crucifixion by adding the discussion between Jesus and the two thieves crucified beside him. Near the end he still found the strength to tell God, "Into your hands I commit my spirit." One might hope that a gay vision of the Passion would show Jesus speaking from the cross to the man he loved, but the viewer is denied such comfort here. In Blanchard's vision, there are neither thieves nor family to talk with Jesus. He hangs alone.

The dying Jesus was not depicted at all in Christianity's first millennium.

The very name of Blanchard's crucifixion—*Jesus Dies*—expresses the modern spirit of the image. The dying Jesus was not depicted at all in Christianity's first millennium. The cross is one of the world's most common symbols now, but crucifixion images are not the only or even the original way to worship Jesus. Christians drew strength from the crucifixion story in the era of early Christian martyrs, but back then artists had to disguise crosses as anchors or tridents to avoid Roman persecution. After Christianity gained legal status in 313, a few images began to appear with the Christ on the cross, but he was vibrantly alive, head held high in victory over death. The Passion was always depicted with the resurrection as one unified triumph. But mostly the cross was absent until the 10th century. The way Jesus died was not very important to his followers. For a thousand years Christian art usually celebrated Jesus as the Good Shepherd or the ruler of God's bountiful creation. The risen Christ brought life and abundance. During this period the church was fairly tolerant of homosexuality and even honored queer love through paired same-sex saints, "brother-making" commitment ceremonies for male couples, and homoerotic devotional imagery.

A shift began when the church joined forces with political and military powers near the end of Christianity's first millennium. The oldest surviving crucifix with a dead Jesus is the Gero Cross from 970. The life-sized wooden sculpture was carved by the descendants of Saxons who survived vicious military campaigns led by Charlemagne. The Pope crowned him as Holy Roman Emperor in 800, and soon he forced Christianity upon the native cultures of Europe. In what is now Germany, Charlemagne's armies killed or deported thousands of Saxons and chopped down the sacred tree of their indigenous religion.

As the centuries passed, Jesus' death on the cross was portrayed with increasing intensity and realism. Crucifixion scenes spread across Europe, along with a new theology of atonement. Christians were urged to imagine themselves at the foot of the cross and to contemplate Christ's agony as he was killed to atone for their own particular sins. People who felt guilty for killing Jesus were less likely to resist domination. The Gero Cross expressed the anguish of a conquered people, but it also served to normalize violence. Leaders expanded their use of religion to justify bloodshed with the first Crusade in 1095. Eventually the death scene was enshrined as the 12th Station on the Way of the Cross.

As crucifixion art proliferated, hostility began to be directed specifically at same-sex erotic behavior. In 1120 the Council of Nablus established punishments for sodomy, setting a new precedent in medieval church law. Then came campaigns against heresy, which often used the terms "heresy" and "sodomy" interchangeably. The church directly or indirectly caused the execution of thousands for homosexuality over the next 700 years. Witch burning occurred in the same period and claimed the lives of countless lesbian women whose non-conformity was condemned as witchcraft. Blanchard says that their modern counterparts—LGBT people murdered in gay bashings, driven to suicide, or killed by AIDS—were on his mind as he painted *Jesus Dies*.

The crucifixion of Christ became so crucial that it was portrayed by virtually every artist in the Renaissance and Baroque eras, including Michelangelo, Da Vinci, and Rembrandt. One of the most influential versions may also be the most horrific: the Isenheim Altarpiece. German artist Matthias Grünewald created it around 1505. He portrays a ghastly, emaciated Jesus writhing in pain, his body covered with oozing sores. Like it or not, such graphic crucifixions still fascinate 21st-centuries sensibilities, as shown by the popularity of director Mel Gibson's brutally violent 2004 film *The Passion of the Christ*.

Christian art has been largely eclipsed by secular imagery in the modern era, with important exceptions. Some famous 20th-century artists still used the crucifixion motif to symbolize cruelty and sacrifice, convey emotion, and critique society. Russian avant-garde painter Marc Chagall emphasized Jesus' Jewish identity to call attention to Nazi persecution in his expressionist *White Crucifixion*. Picasso painted a cubist crucifixion and surrealist Salvador Dali hung Jesus on a multi-dimensional cross in *Crucifixion (Corpus Hypercubus)*. Others made political statements by changing the setting or substituting the standard Jesus with a variety of different figures. For example, German artist George Grosz was tried for blasphemy in the 1920s for his anti-military drawing of the crucified Christ in a gas mask, captioned, "Shut up and obey!" British artist Edwina Sandys caused an international uproar by sculpting a female *Christa* in 1975. Blanchard's gay Passion series has also been attacked by conservatives as "perverted" and "blasphemous."

The horrors of the cross resonate with LGBT experience. The crucifixion naturally became the most common subject in contemporary queer Christian art because queer people have been scapegoated, abused, and killed, often for religious reasons. Some contemporary artists have made the crucified Christ explicitly gay, confirming that God identifies totally with queer suffering. They have photographed the crucifixion with contemporary LGBT models. They have changed the location to gay cruising areas or AIDS wards, showing how the marginalization of gay men led them to literally die for their sexuality. Atlanta painter Becki Jayne Harrelson and New Mexico iconographer William Hart McNichols placed a "faggot" sign on the cross over his head. Brazilian cartoonist Carlos Latuff wrapped him in a rainbow loincloth. Photographers Elisabeth Ohlson Wallin of Sweden and Fernando Bayona Gonzalez of Spain, working separately, each did a Life of Christ series where the crucifixion scene shows Jesus lying spread-eagle on the ground after a gay bashing. Mary Button of Tennessee pairs the crucifixion of Christ with the murder of a transgender woman. Blanchard takes a more subtle approach. There are no overt gay references in his crucifixion. The viewer needs to consider the subtitle and other paintings in the series to know that this is a "gay vision."

Blanchard shows the crucifixion for what it was—one man's violent death. Like prophets and freedom fighters of every age, Jesus was killed for challenging the status quo. The man who loves too much must die. By witnessing the crucifixion with compassion, viewers can stand symbolically beside all who suffer. They can face their own suffering without losing hope by seeing it in a larger context. The body of Christ represents the Oneness that goes by many names. The god-man dies and God's identification with humanity, including gay humanity, is complete. ●

Like prophets and freedom fighters of every age, Jesus was killed for challenging the status quo.

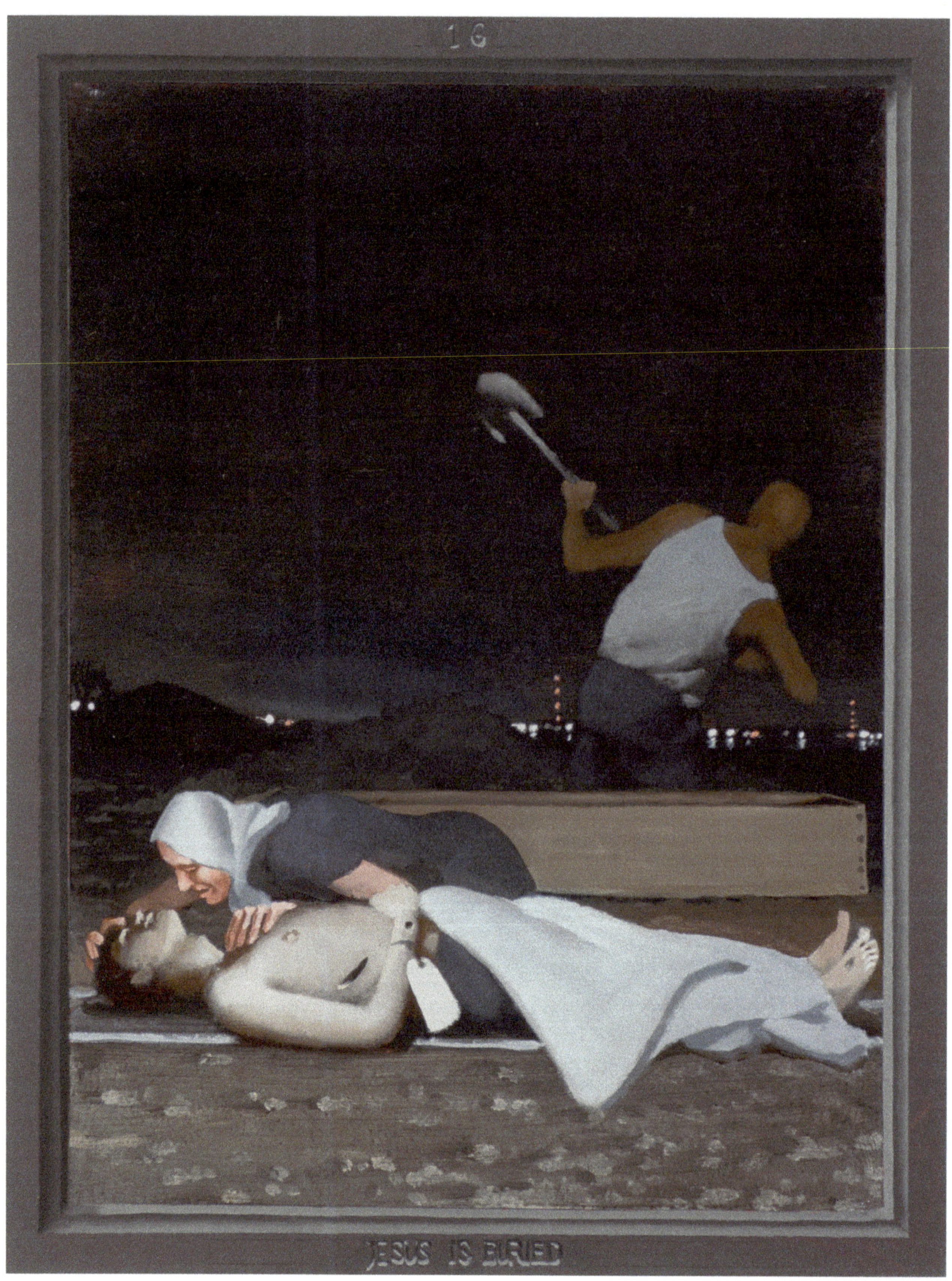

COLLECTION OF PAUL BRIDGEWATER

16. Jesus is Buried

"They took the body of Jesus, and bound it in linen cloths with the spices, as is the burial custom." —John 19:40

A mother mourns her dead son in *Jesus is Buried*. A gravedigger shovels dirt while city lights glimmer in the distance. Mary leans over the body of Jesus, ready to kiss his ashen face goodbye. Crucifixion wounds are still visible on his wrists, feet, and side. An identification tag from a morgue is tied around his wrist. His corpse is bloodless and wrapped in a plain white shroud. A modest wooden coffin waits.

The simple dignity of the scene conveys the deepest sorrow and the finality of death. The burial of Jesus is described in all four gospels and discussed in the epistles, the earliest summaries of the Christian message. His burial has been important to Christians since Biblical times because it confirms that Jesus really died, thus laying the groundwork for the miracle of his resurrection. The Bible reports that Jesus was laid in a rock-hewn tomb with the help of his disciple Joseph of Arimathea, while Mary Magdalene and "the other Mary" watched.

The subject is common in art history, where it is known as the Lamentation. Like most scenes from the Passion, the Lamentation was not depicted at all until the 11th century, and then proliferated in the Renaissance and Baroque periods. A notable version was painted by Italian Renaissance artist Andrea Mantegna, who showed Jesus' foreshortened cadaver on a slab, wounded feet first. The last two scenes in the traditional Stations of the Cross depict Jesus being taken down from the cross and buried in his tomb.

Nothing touched Renaissance viewers more deeply than a mother's grief, so artists gave an increasingly central role to Mary. They focused on the heart-rending moment when the bereaved mother cradles her son's dead body in a specific type of Lamentation known as a Pieta (Italian for "pity"). The most famous Pieta is the sculpture by Michelangelo at St. Peter's Basilica in Vatican City. It has become one of the Passion's most iconic scenes, often copied or parodied. Modern artists have relocated it or switched the characters to make a political statement. German Surrealist Max Ernst used it to depict the unconscious mind. He replaced Jesus and Mary with a self-portrait of the artist held by his staunchly Catholic father in *Pieta or Revolution by Night*.

Some versions of the Lamentation address the impact of AIDS and homophobia on queer people. The magnitude of the AIDS death toll was made worse by Christians who saw the disease as God's punishment for homosexuality. In her famous *Ecce Homo* series, Swedish artist Elisabeth Ohlson Wallin photographed an emaciated gay AIDS patient cradled by a leather bar employee in the AIDS ward of a Stockholm hospital. American painter Matthew Wettlaufer's *Pieta* shows a gay man at the bedside of his dying lover while bombs drop and a blanket lists the names of war-torn countries and gay-bashing victims. *Stations of the Cross: The Struggle for LGBT Equality* by Mary Button weaves together past and present to make deadly comparisons: Jesus is taken down from his cross beside a map of states banning same-sex marriage, and he is laid in his tomb under the watchful gaze of LGBT youths who were driven to suicide.

Blanchard's understated Lamentation is closely related to the next two paintings in his gay vision of the Passion. All three images use dark tones to convey Jesus' experiences with death and the underworld. Life, not death, was the focus of Jesus' ministry, and he gave mixed messages about mourning the dead. He promised comfort for those who mourn. He was so concerned about the welfare of his bereaved mother and his beloved disciple that from the cross he declared them to be family for each other. But he did not have an overly sentimental attachment to family or funeral customs. He even ordered a disciple to skip his father's funeral, saying, "Leave the dead to bury their own dead." ●

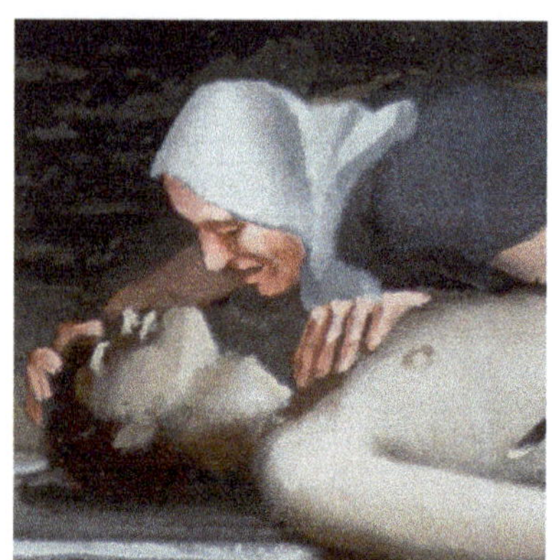

Jesus promised comfort for those who mourn.

"You are dust, and to dust you shall return." —Genesis 3:19

After Jesus died, the authorities allowed one of his friends to take his body for burial. Almost all of his many supporters were gone. Jesus' body was laid to rest in a fresh tomb at sundown, just before the Sabbath began. When they buried him, they also buried a beautiful part of themselves. Sometimes the humiliations continue even after death… when homophobes picket the funerals of LGBT people and other targets, when mortuaries refuse to handle the bodies of AIDS patients, when families exclude same-sex partners from memorial services, on and on. Jesus understood grief and didn't try to suppress it. He said, Blessed are those who mourn, for they will be comforted.

Jesus, I wait in silence at your grave.

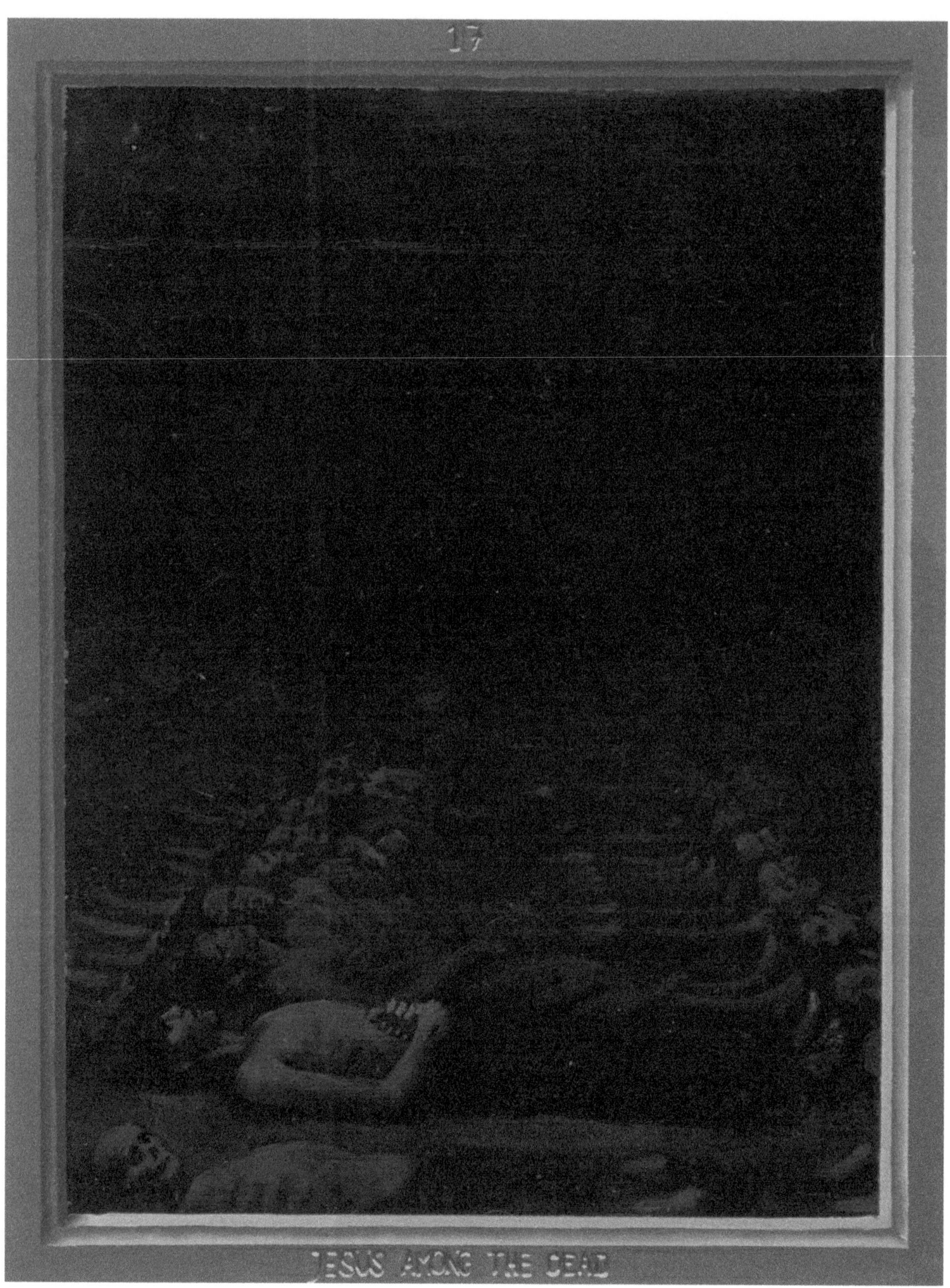

COLLECTION OF ROBERT WILDER NIGHTINGALE

17. Jesus Among the Dead

"He poured out his soul to death, and was numbered with the transgressors." —Isaiah 53:12

Endless rows of corpses fill a vast black space in *Jesus Among the Dead.* Even in death, Jesus is not separate from humanity. He lies with the skeletons, the dead bodies, and the stink—a common man in a common grave. Jesus can be identified by his crucifixion wounds. His corpse only stands out because it has not begun to decompose. He glows just slightly with a sick luminescence. Jesus just lies there, not judging, not rescuing, not rising. He is simply present with people in the darkest state of being. This must be hell, or some human holocaust. Perhaps there is no difference.

At first glance Blanchard's painting looks almost entirely black. The painting challenges viewers to keep looking until their eyes adjust to the lack of light. Then shapes and meanings emerge from the shadows to offer uncomfortable wisdom from the depths. Mystical traditions say there is power to be gained by descent into the dark netherworld of dreams, intuition, death, and the unknown. In the mass grave Jesus is fulfilling Isaiah's prophecy that God's Suffering Servant would be buried with "transgressors" and "the wicked." The black void conveys utter despair over the meaninglessness of life.

The Bible doesn't tell what Jesus experienced in the interlude between crucifixion and resurrection, but artists and theologians of the past were quick to fill the void. The Apostle's Creed clearly states, "He descended into hell," or in another translation, "He descended to the dead." Artists traditionally show Jesus leading an uprising in the realm of the dead. The subject is known as the Anastasis or Harrowing of Hell, when Christ descends to hell or limbo to rescue the souls held captive there since the

"Even the darkness is not dark to you." —Psalm 139:12*

Like all human beings, Jesus eventually had to die. In effect, it was like he was buried in a mass grave with all humankind: Saints and sinners, queer and straight, male and female, all of us without exception, even the worst of us. His body rested in peace with the other corpses. Jesus lay buried like a seed waiting in the wintry earth. He didn't believe death was the end. During his lifetime, he often talked about the afterlife. He said he would always be with us, connected like a vine to a branch. But when his body lay cold in the tomb, his friends and family simply missed him.

O God, can these bones live?

beginning of time. The subject arose in Byzantine culture and then spread to the West around the eighth century. Some churches mark the event on Holy Saturday by stripping their altars bare or covering them with black cloth.

Blanchard's Jesus stays utterly dead in the afterlife, sharing the reality of human powerlessness. He is not triumphantly waking the deceased, at least not yet. A few artists, notably German Renaissance painter Hans Holbein, depicted the corpse of Jesus with gruesome realism. But Blanchard's monolithically black visual vocabulary in *Jesus Among the Dead* has more in common with modern art, photography, and philosophy. He based the composition on documentary photographs of the Holocaust, especially photos of bodies laid out in long rows after the liberation of the Nazi concentration camp at Nordhausen in 1945. New Mexico gallery owner Robert Wilder Nightingale singled out *Jesus Among the Dead* to purchase for his private collection when it was exhibited in Taos in 2007. "To me the work is haunting. A nightmare I wish never to see happen in reality," he explained.

This is one of the most difficult paintings in Blanchard's Passion series because it's hard to see anything at all in the gloom. It resembles the all-black abstract paintings done by American abstract artist Ad Reinhardt in the 1960s. Reinhardt claimed that they were the "last paintings that anyone can paint," a fitting concept for Jesus among the dead. Reinhardt painted them in the era when the "God is dead" theological movement announced that there was no longer any cultural relevance for the idea of a transcendent God acting in human history. Another precedent for Blanchard's black image is the Vietnam Veterans Memorial Wall in Washington DC. Inscribed with a seemingly endless list of war casualties, the memorial wall stretches like a long, black gash in the earth.

The most significant memorial for many in the LGBT community is the Names Project AIDS Memorial Quilt. More than 48,000 handmade panels commemorate those who died of AIDS, including thousands of gay men. Before effective treatments were developed in the 1990s, AIDS was stigmatized as the "gay plague" and the LGBT community felt like a war zone as thousands died. Fundamentalists preached that AIDS was God's punishment for homosexuality and President Reagan kept silent. Lovers, friends, and family learned to show they cared by staying present with the dying. Meanwhile they advocated change through groups such as ACT UP, whose motto was "Silence = Death." There are many hells in which people are trapped neither fully alive nor dead.

The AIDS pandemic is part of a larger queer holocaust. Many LGBT people experience a kind of legal limbo and even a living death, trapped in the private hell of the closet. Some have wished themselves dead and even taken their own lives. Those who wore the pink triangle were exterminated in Nazi death camps. The tragic history of church-approved persecution for homosexuality stretches back to the 13th century, when the first "sodomites" were burned at the stake. In Blanchard's vision, Jesus rests with them in the ashes. ●

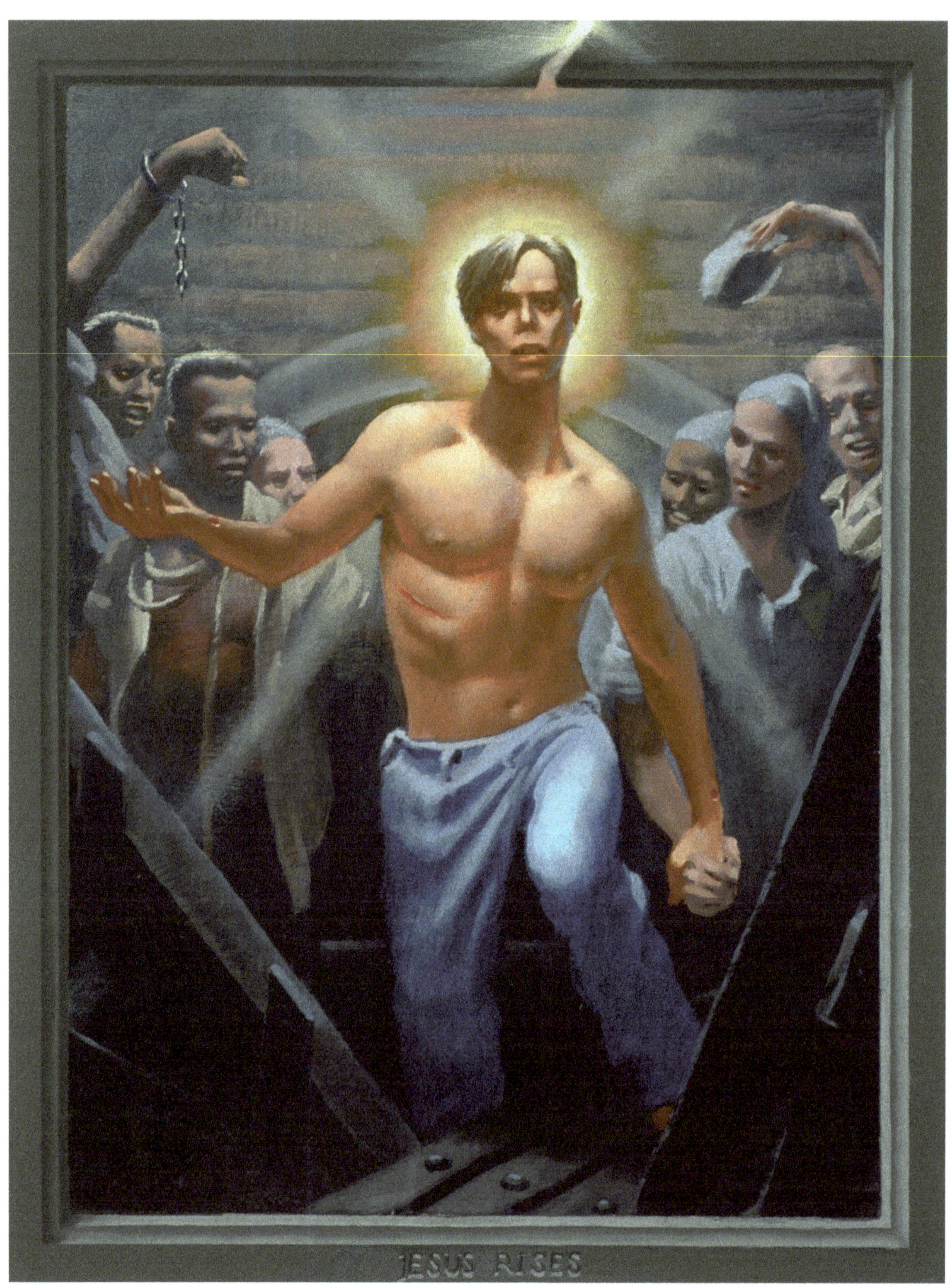

COLLECTION OF KITTREDGE CHERRY AND AUDREY LOCKWOOD

18. Jesus Rises

"For if we have been united with him in a death like his,
we shall certainly be united with him in a resurrection like his." —Romans 6:5

A handsome young prisoner in blue jeans leads a joyous jailbreak in *Jesus Rises*. He holds hands with another inmate as he steps upward, leading the captives to freedom. Jesus still bears the wounds of his crucifixion, but he glows with life and health. For the first time in this series, Jesus also emits a halo. Beams of light shoot from his head in four directions, forming a diagonal cross behind him. Jesus does not bask in his own glory, but is determined to use his new-found power to free others. Christ is even more powerful as a liberator because he is also one of the prisoners. His inner light illuminates the shadowy crowd behind him.

Blanchard dares to paint a communal resurrection. It does not occur in a vacuum or even in a lonely cave. His Jesus is no isolated individual experiencing a one-of-a-kind miracle, but first in the diverse group that will become the body of Christ in the world. One prisoner raises a fist in victory, a broken chain dangling from his shackled wrist. Another waves his hat in celebration. The scene can be read as "gay" because Jesus appears to hold hands with another man. He heads directly for the viewer, making eye contact, ready to burst through the flat surface of the image. The arch motif recurs in the brick wall behind them, but this time Jesus rises above it. Even the picture frame cannot hold back the risen Christ. The frame cracks open at the top as light breaks through in this naturalistic yet supernatural scene. The words painted on the inseparable faux frame inform the viewer that this is the moment of cosmic significance when "Jesus Rises." He overcomes death itself in an updated vision of the first Easter.

The resurrection is the most unacceptable part of the Passion story for most modern people, who mistrust miracles and are suspicious of happy endings. Artists and theologians struggle to reconcile a realistic understanding of the human condition with hope for the best. Skeptics question whether the resurrection really happened, but it is central to the faith of most Christians. Easter is when Jesus becomes more than a great teacher, when minds are challenged to stretch and take a leap of faith. By rising from the dead Jesus embodies a mystery that saves a broken world. Death ceases to be a prison and becomes a passage to new life. Love is stronger than death.

Jesus was a unique historical person, but he also epitomizes the archetype of the god-man hero who returns from the dead with new powers to help others. There are many ancient myths of gods who die and return, sometimes in harmony with the seasons. Cycles of death and rebirth repeat in nature and in the hearts of people who let parts of themselves "die" in order to grow. Christ lives again through the actions of countless martyrs, prophets, and humanitarians throughout history up to the present. Jesus triumphs not by denying death, but by moving through it, drawing energy from multiple dimensions. Ultimately he unites birth and death in himself.

Illustrating the resurrection has always been a challenge for artists. The Bible doesn't describe the actual moment when Jesus rose from the dead, but instead conveys the good news with reports of the empty tomb and appearances of the risen Christ. For more than a thousand years artists followed suit and avoided depicting the resurrection itself. Even the traditional Stations of the Cross stops short of the resurrection. The subject became more common in art starting in the twelfth century. At first Jesus was shown stepping out of a Roman-style sarcophagus. Then artists began to picture Christ hovering in the air. The 16th-century Isenheim Altarpiece by Matthias Grünewald matches its horrific crucifixion with an equally extreme resurrection in which a radiantly robust Jesus floats above his tomb, sublimely awake with arms lifted high. But church authorities clamped down on the trend, insisting that Jesus' feet must remain firmly on the ground. Renaissance artist Leonardo Da Vinci pioneered a more natural approach with Jesus emerging from a rock-hewn cave.

Usually Jesus rises alone, perhaps accompanied by angels and bowling over or even trampling upon the Roman guards outside his tomb. Blanchard's group scene has a lot in common with another artistic tradition. Artists show Jesus rescuing the souls of the dead in a scene known as the Harrowing of Hell, but that is usually a separate event before the resurrection. Blanchard cites English Romantic artist William Blake as a visual source for some of his resurrection and post-resurrection imagery.

Jesus Rises spoke to me from the moment I first saw it, and my appreciation for it has grown over the years as I shared it and discussed it with others. The original *Jesus Rises* hangs in my own home, a gift from the artist. Blanchard wanted me to have the painting because it is what originally brought us together. In 2005 I was hunting for queer Christian images for my JesusInLove.org website, which was still in the design stage. It was hard to find any kind of LGBT-oriented Christ figures, but the rarest of all was the queer resurrection. I rejoiced when an Internet search finally led me to Blanchard's *Jesus Rises*. As I explained in my first letter to him, "I am very eager to include *Jesus Rises* in particular because I believe that Jesus' Resurrection is an essential part of his

"I am the resurrection and the life." —John 11:25

Christ lives! Nobody knows exactly how it happened, but Jesus rose to new life on the third day after his crucifixion. The mystery of resurrection replaced the law of cause and effect with a new reality: the law of love. Jesus lives in our hearts now. Just as he promised, he freed people from all forms of bondage. Captives are released from every prison. LGBT people are free to leave every closet of shame. Christ glows with the colors of all beings. People of all kinds—queer and straight, old and young, male and female and everything in between, of every race and age and ability—together we are the body of Christ.

Jesus, welcome back!

story. I have managed to find some gay- and lesbian-oriented images of Jesus, but most focus on his humanity, while your *Jesus Rises* succeeds in showing how flesh and spirit can go together in a gay context." After some discussion, he agreed to let me use it on my website. Later I shared more of his Passion series in my book *Art That Dares* and a 2007 exhibit that I helped organize at JHS Gallery in Taos. *Jesus Rises* is displayed in my living room, where it serves as a constant reminder to maintain hope no matter what happens.

Later I did locate a few other LGBT-oriented resurrection images. Jesus comes back from the dead as the U.S. Supreme Court rules for marriage equality in the 2013 painting that completes the series *Stations of the Cross: The Struggle For LGBT Equality* by Mary Button of Tennessee. Welsh artist Andrew Craig Williams shows the silhouette of Jesus walking out of his tomb toward a rainbow of light in *Queer Resurrection*, which he created for the Jesus in Love Blog in 2012. New Mexico painter Delmas Howe ends his *Stations* series with *Triumph*, a nude man at New York's gay sex piers with hands upraised in the classic pose of a risen Christ.

Jesus rises in Blanchard's Passion to lead an uprising, as much insurrection as resurrection. He frees people from a prison that can stand for any kind of limitation, including the closets of shame where LGBT people hide. The struggle to reconcile the resurrection with harsh realities can be especially tough for LGBT people who have endured hate crimes, discrimination, and the ravages of the AIDS epidemic. The risen Christ leads the way to a state of being where hate does not always cause more hate, and anger becomes a motivation for life, not destruction. ●

The risen Christ leads the way to a state of being where anger becomes a motivation for life, not destruction.

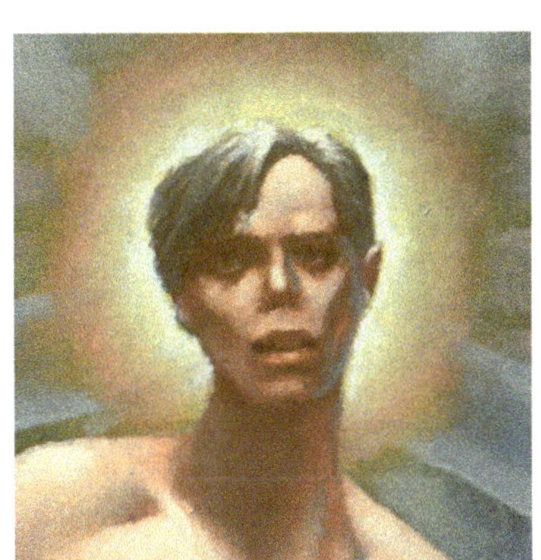

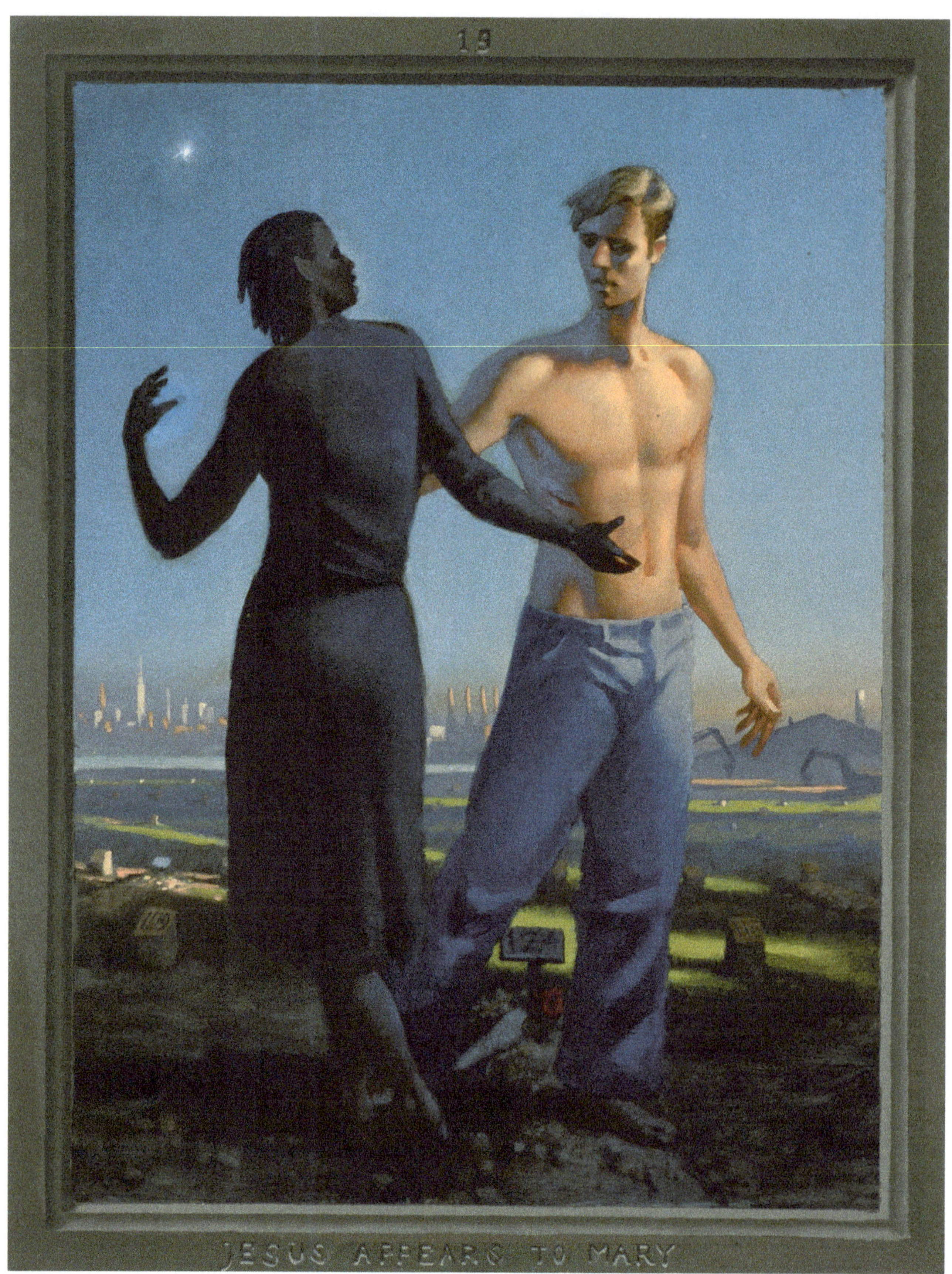

COLLECTION OF THE ARTIST

19. Jesus Appears to Mary

"When he rose early on the first day of the week,
he appeared first to Mary Magdalene." —Mark 16:9

Two friends have a happy reunion at sunrise in *Jesus Appears to Mary*. It almost looks like Jesus is dancing with his own shadow. They circle each other as Mary Magdalene gestures with joyful surprise at finding Jesus alive in the graveyard. A patch of sunlight catches the risen Christ, now restored to health and handsome in his blue jeans. Mary, a black woman, remains in darkness with her back to the viewer. The morning star shines in a gorgeous blue sky while the first rays of dawn awaken the spring-green grass. The frame itself is green—even the faux wood has sprung to life!

On the distant horizon are excavating machines. A body of water separates Jesus and Mary from the faraway city skyline. They are surrounded by numbered gravestones. The one behind Jesus is marked "124." It is the same number on the mysterious tag around Jesus' neck in the first painting of this series. The artist has stated that he chose "124" because it has no special meaning in Christianity. His Jesus died with a random number, a human castoff stripped of his name. The gravestones and setting look like Hart Island, a public cemetery for the unknown and indigent in New York City. Operated by prison labor, Hart Island is the world's largest tax-funded cemetery, with daily mass burials and almost a million bodies buried there.

First Mary was blinded by grief, and then she saw a deeper truth: The living Christ is here now. It was an "aha moment" when sudden clarity led to life-changing insight. The dynamic tension between the figures suggests that this is the incident known as *Noli me tangere*. The Latin phrase is usually translated as "Don't touch me." Jesus spoke the words to

“Why do you seek the living among the dead?” — Luke 24:5

Mary Magdalene went to the tomb of Jesus early on Sunday morning. It was empty! She started crying and someone came up to her. Mary thought he was the gardener until he spoke her name. Her heart leaped as she recognized Jesus. Human beings often miss the presence of God right in front of us. Like Mary, we get lost in our emotions. It feels like God is far away or even dead. Then something happens and suddenly we know: God was with us all along. Jesus chose an unlikely person as the first witness to his resurrection. Women were second-class citizens in the time of Jesus, not unlike LGBT people in many places today. But Jesus, who loved outcasts, gladly revealed himself to the woman who came for him. Christ is ready to speak to each of us by name, even if we are looking in all the wrong places.

Jesus, where are you now?
Will you speak to me?

Mary Magdalene in John 20:17 when they met after his resurrection. In John's gospel, Mary went to visit Jesus' tomb before sunrise on Easter. She was distraught that his corpse was missing—until the risen Christ called her by name. Overcome with emotion, she started to hug him, but he stopped her with a request that has multiple translations. The original Greek is best rendered as "Stop clinging to me." He explained that he didn't want her to hang on to him because he had not yet "ascended." The scene has been an iconographic standard for artists throughout the Christian world since late antiquity. Modern artists are still keen to portray the suffering and death of Jesus, but most won't touch the subject of his resurrection. Some indirect references continue in works such as Picasso's mysterious 1903 allegorical painting *La Vie*, the masterpiece of his Blue Period. It includes references to *Noli Me Tangere* by Renaissance painter Antonio da Correggio.

Jesus' appearance to Mary is good news for all who are disenfranchised, including today's LGBT people. Jesus chose a woman as the first witness to his resurrection in an era when women weren't even allowed to testify at legal proceedings. Mary Magdalene has an undeserved reputation for sexual sins. The church mistakenly labeled her as a prostitute for centuries, but the Bible does not support this view. Progressive theologians are reclaiming her as a role model for church leaders. The Bible portrays Mary Magdalene as the most important woman follower of Jesus. She supported his ministry with her resources, traveled with him on his teaching tours, witnessed his crucifixion, and hurried to his tomb before sunrise. In Luke's gospel angels ask Mary Magdalene and the other women at the empty tomb: "Why do you seek the living among the dead?" LGBT Christians and allies sometimes ask themselves the same question as they seek the living Christ in the rusty, deadening rituals and rules of the institutional church. ●

Jesus' appearance to Mary is good news for all who are disenfranchised, including today's LGBT people.

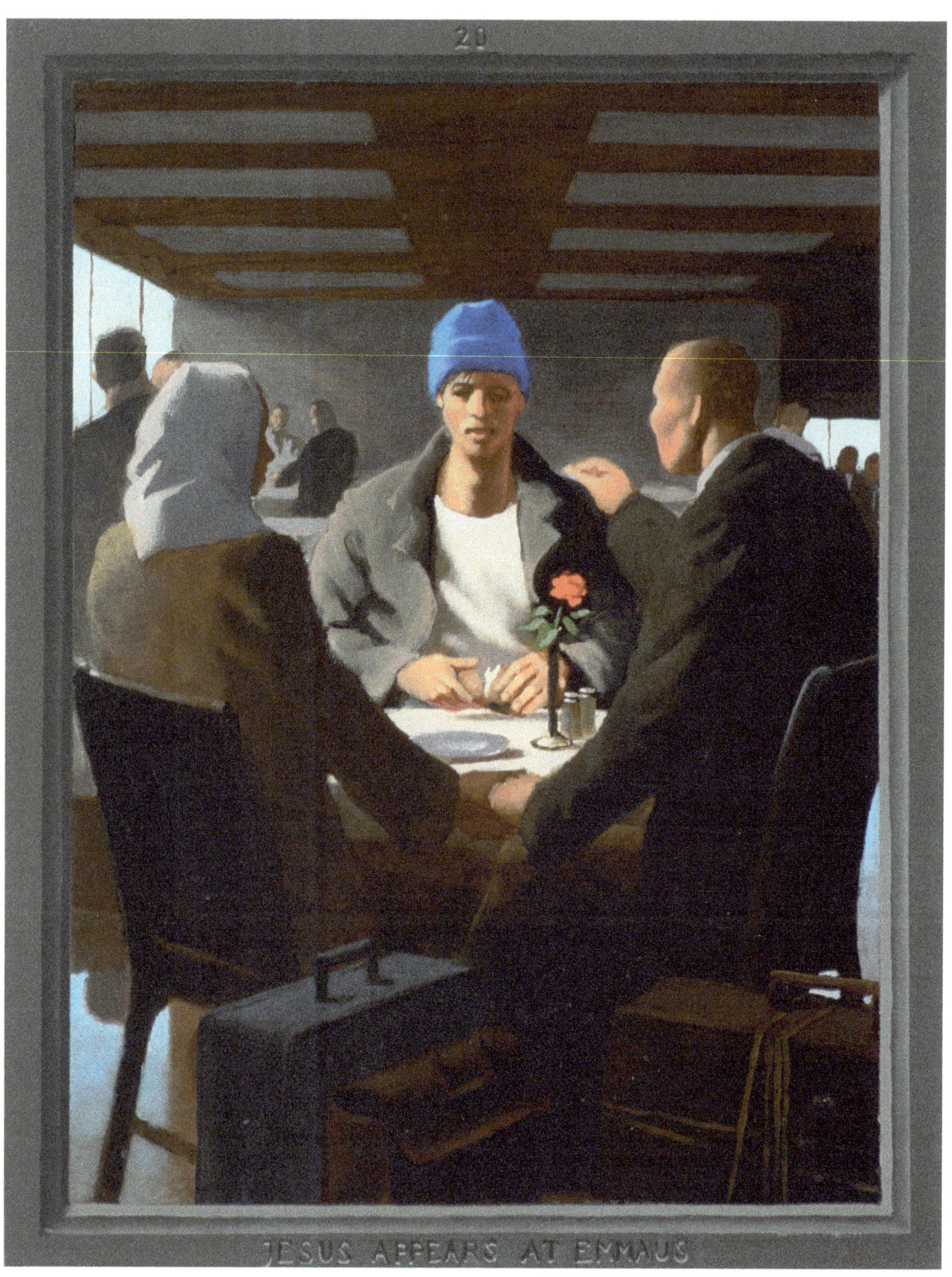

COLLECTION OF JODI AND MICHAEL SIMMONS

20. Jesus Appears at Emmaus

"When he was at table with them, he took the bread and blessed, and broke it, and gave it to them. And their eyes were opened and they recognized him." —Luke 24:30-31

Three travelers share a meal together in *Jesus Appears at Emmaus*. Jesus is hard to identify with his hair hidden under a bright blue ski cap. He sits at a restaurant table, breaking a loaf of bread. His companions, a man and a woman, touch in an attitude of prayer. The setting looks like an airport lounge with large windows. The table is nicely set with a red rose and generic salt and pepper shakers. Suitcases in the foreground confirm that they are traveling. It is a normal scene of friends eating together, until the viewer recognizes Jesus. And that is the point.

The painting illustrates the Biblical story of two disciples who met the risen Christ on the road, but didn't recognize him at first. A disciple named Cleopas and his unnamed companion encountered the stranger on the way to Emmaus, a village seven miles from Jerusalem. They confided in him about their sadness over Jesus' crucifixion and the disappearance of his corpse. The mysterious stranger listened and comforted them by using scripture to explain what happened. Impressed, the disciples persuaded him to join them for supper in Emmaus. When the stranger blessed and broke the bread, they suddenly recognized Jesus.

The Emmaus story fits the mythic pattern of the magical traveling companion who appears unexpectedly and offers help. Such legends were common in medieval Europe when the practice of pilgrimage was important and widespread. Artists have been depicting the Emmaus events since the fifth century, but in the Middle Ages they began to give more attention to the encounter on the road. Jesus wore a large pilgrim's hat to explain why his disciples failed to identify him. Pilgrimage fell out of favor in the 16th century with the Reformation. Then the supper scene, with all its Eucharistic implications, became increasingly prevalent. Artists began to focus on the dramatic moment of recognition, with famous versions painted by Rembrandt in the Netherlands and Caravaggio in Italy. In modern times the supper at Emmaus has lost much of its appeal to artists.

Artists of the past generally assumed that both disciples at Emmaus were male, but Blanchard brings the episode into the present and makes one disciple female, subtly communicating that gender does not limit a person's relationship with God. The woman wears a headscarf, perhaps a hijab. Jesus may be sharing a meal with Muslim refugees. That possibility is especially powerful because Blanchard painted his Passion series in the aftermath of 9/11 attacks by Islamic terrorists. He strategically places the red rose so it blooms over Jesus' heart, echoing the Sacred Heart motif in which Jesus exposes his physical heart as a symbol of his love and sacrifice. The mood and style of Blanchard's Emmaus are reminiscent of 20th-century American painter Edward Hopper. Like Hopper, Blanchard finds poetry in an anonymous urban environment, capturing the elusive interaction of people in a quiet moment just before something happens.

In the Bible, Jesus disappears as soon as he is recognized.

Blanchard's Emmaus painting now hangs in the kitchen of Jodi and Michael Simmons. They owned JHS Gallery in Taos, New Mexico, when Blanchard's gay Passion series was displayed there in a 2007 group show. "We purchased the painting because we felt it most accurately captured the spirit of what we intended by the entire exhibition *Who Do You Say That I Am? Visions of Christ, Gender, and Justice,*" Jodi explained. "The Supper at Emmaus has always been one of both Michael and my favorite Gospel stories. I think it is the best example of 'mature' Christianity. Life is a journey; we meet many travelers and experiences along the way. To be able to be clear and awake enough to recognize the Light and Presence of God in all places, with all people, is a great, great milestone. Michael and I both think that it is absolutely the best image of this difficult to convey spiritual reality that we have ever seen."

The Emmaus story has particular parallels with the queer spiritual journey. Even devout Christians may be blind to the sacred worth of LGBT people. The travelers at Emmaus can also be compared to LGBT people who turn their backs on their churches of origin—and then find God on the outside. In the Bible narrative Jesus disappears as soon as he is recognized. The disciples return immediately to the early Christian community in Jerusalem to tell what happened. Likewise, some LGBT people leave the church and go back later to proclaim their fresh understanding of the all-inclusive Christ. ●

"Where two or three are gathered in my name, **there am I** in the midst of them."

—Matthew 18:20

Two travelers met a stranger on the way to a village called Emmaus. While on the road they told the stranger about Jesus: the hopes he had stirred in them, his horrific execution, and Mary's unbelievable story that he was still alive. Their hearts burned as the stranger reframed it for them, quoting the ancient prophets and putting it in a larger context. They convinced him to stay and join them for dinner in Emmaus. As the meal began, he blessed the bread and gave it to them. It was one of those moments when the presence of God breaks through ordinary life. Suddenly they saw: The stranger was Jesus! He had been with them all along. LGBT people are strangers in too many churches. It may be difficult for some Christians to perceive God's image in queer lives. People can also be blind to their own sacred worth. But at any moment, the grace of an unexpected encounter can open our eyes.

Come and travel with me, Jesus.
Or are you already here?

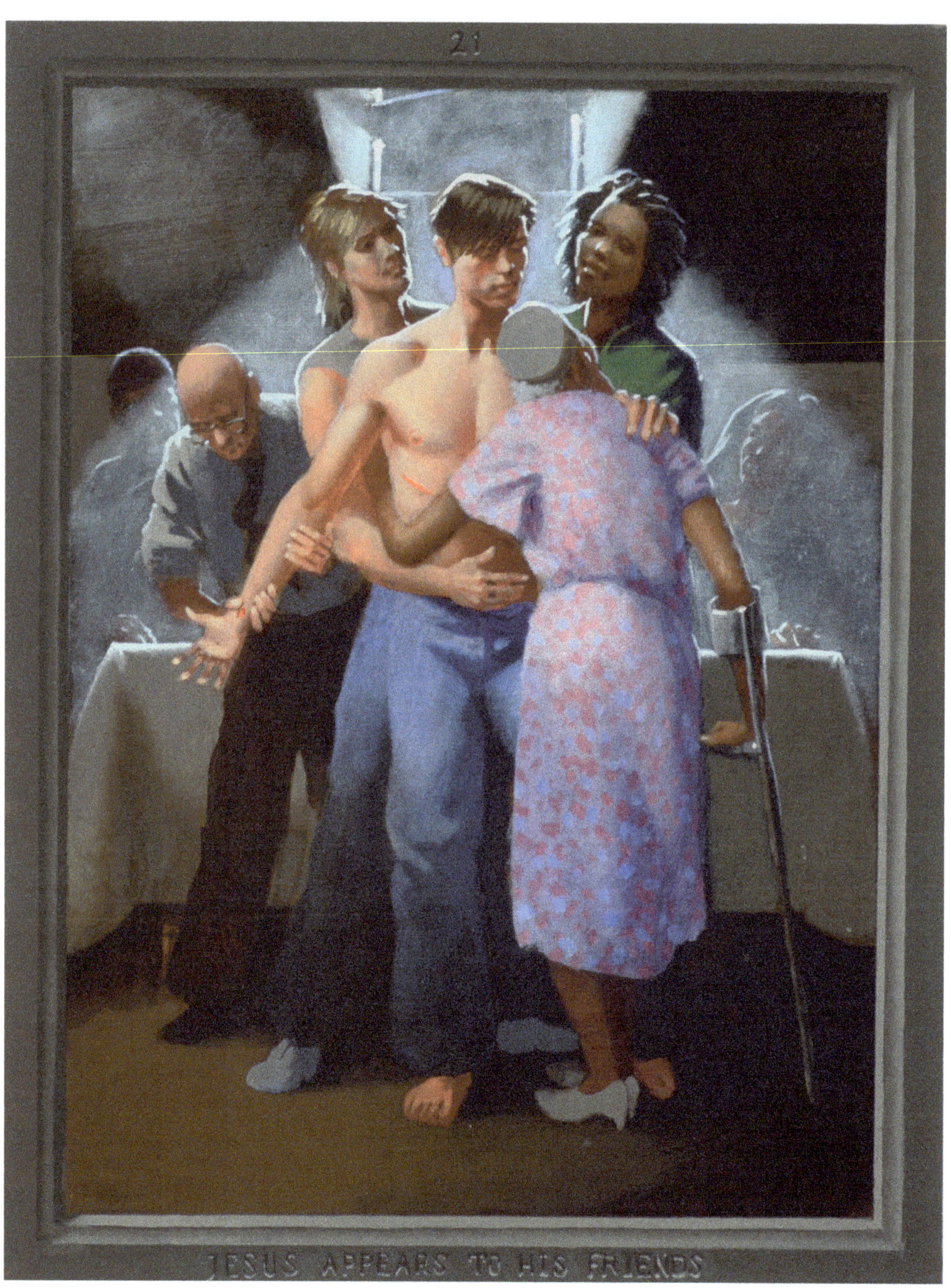

COLLECTION OF BILL CARPENTER

21. Jesus Appears to His Friends

"See my hands and my feet, that it is I myself; handle me, and see." —Luke 24:39

Friends react with joy—and some doubt—to the return of the risen Christ in *Jesus Appears to His Friends*. Jesus allows himself to be embraced and examined by his diverse friendship group. He gets hugs from his beloved disciple and an elderly black woman with a cane. Smiling beside them is a young black woman, apparently Mary Magdalene. Meanwhile a bald skeptic in a suit inspects his wounded wrist. Other disciples watch from behind. The red gash in Jesus' side stands out against his manly physique.

Everyone in Blanchard's painting is delighted to see Jesus, except the bald Doubting Thomas figure in the tie and glasses. Jesus affirms the believers, but doesn't push away the pragmatist who is busy fact-checking. He is welcome to check the wounds scientifically. Thomas provides a positive role model as someone who engages with religion without falling for any mystical trickery. Many people, queer or otherwise, share the skeptic's desire to develop a belief system based on direct experience and not get caught up in all the hoopla about Christ.

Jesus has been to hell and back. He's managed to return to the land of the living. The same room and some of the same people were pictured in Blanchard's Last Supper, but here the mood is transformed from a dark-toned goodbye to a happy hello, lit up with lavender and with warm flesh tones. Misty moonlight pours in from the back window in the shape of an ascending dove, hinting at the presence of the Holy Spirit.

The Bible offers differing accounts of Jesus' post-resurrection appearances to his friends. Taken as a whole, the gospels describe how the disciples were hiding from authorities behind closed doors when Jesus "came and stood among them." He calmed their fears and

"The doors were shut, but Jesus came and stood among them,
and said, 'Peace be with you.'" —John 20:26

Jesus' friends were hiding together, afraid of the authorities who killed him. The doors were shut, but somehow Jesus got inside and stood among them. They couldn't believe it! He urged them to touch him, and even invited them to inspect the wounds from his crucifixion. As they felt his warm skin, their doubts and fears turned into joy. Jesus liked touch. He often touched people in order to heal them, and he let people touch him. He defied taboos and allowed himself to be touched by women and people with diseases. He understood human sexuality, befriending prostitutes and other sexual outcasts. LGBT people sometimes hide themselves in closets of shame, but Jesus wasn't like that. He was pleased with own human body, even after it was wounded.

Jesus, can I really touch you?

breathed the Holy Spirit upon them. One disciple, Thomas, had rejected earlier reports that Jesus was still alive. "Unless I see in his hands the print of the nails, and place my finger in the mark of the nails, and place my hand in his side, I will not believe," (John 20:25) he insisted. His doubt turned to faith when Jesus invited him to do just that.

As usual in the gay Passion series, Jesus attracts a surprisingly varied group. The imagery and title emphasize that the people around Jesus were not merely his followers. They were his friends. As he told them at the Last Supper, "I have called you friends, for all that I have heard from God I have made known to you." (*John 15:15)

The focus on friendship led Bill Carpenter to acquire this painting when Blanchard's gay Passion series was displayed at the 2007 National Festival of Progressive Spiritual Art in Taos, New Mexico. Carpenter is one of the leaders of Soulforce, a civil-rights group that works to free LGBT people from religious and political oppression. He went to Taos to teach nonviolent resistance as part of the festival. "I chose *Jesus Appears To His Friends* because, through it, I connected with the humanity of Jesus...He had friends! And, because Doug showed Jesus' friends as a beautifully diverse collection of humanity...just like our world... and I felt that Jesus truly welcomed each and every soul into his world...with no qualification or judgment and I wanted to be reminded of that potential within me," Carpenter said.

The painting fits into the long artistic tradition of Doubting Thomas, a common subject at least since the sixth century. Perhaps the most famous version was painted in 1602 by Italian artist Caravaggio with unflinching realism and street people as models. Artists mostly stopped portraying the Doubting Thomas scene after the Baroque period ended in the 18th century, even though his skepticism sums up the spirit of the modern era.

Blanchard contributes to the standard repertoire of Doubting Thomas iconography by putting him in a larger vision of equality where same-sex love has an honored place. Other contemporary gay versions accentuate the homoeroticism of Thomas touching the wound in Jesus' side, as in the *Circus Christi* series by Spanish photographer Fernando Bayona Gonzalez and the *Intimacy with Christ* triptych by British painter Richard Stott. Jesus' connection with lesbians is highlighted by Swedish artist Elisabeth Ohlson Wallin. She photographs today's lesbian clergy meeting the risen Christ, with red crucifixion wounds visible in his hands, in a scene from her *Ecce Homo* series.

In *Jesus Appears to His Friends*, Blanchard affirms themes that are vital to the LGBT community: Friendship, because many have been cut off from their biological families. Touch, because touching someone of the same gender has been taboo. And doubt, because religion has been used to justify violence against LGBT people. Crossing the boundary from death to life, Jesus touches those who live in the borderlands between male and female, between doubt and faith. ●

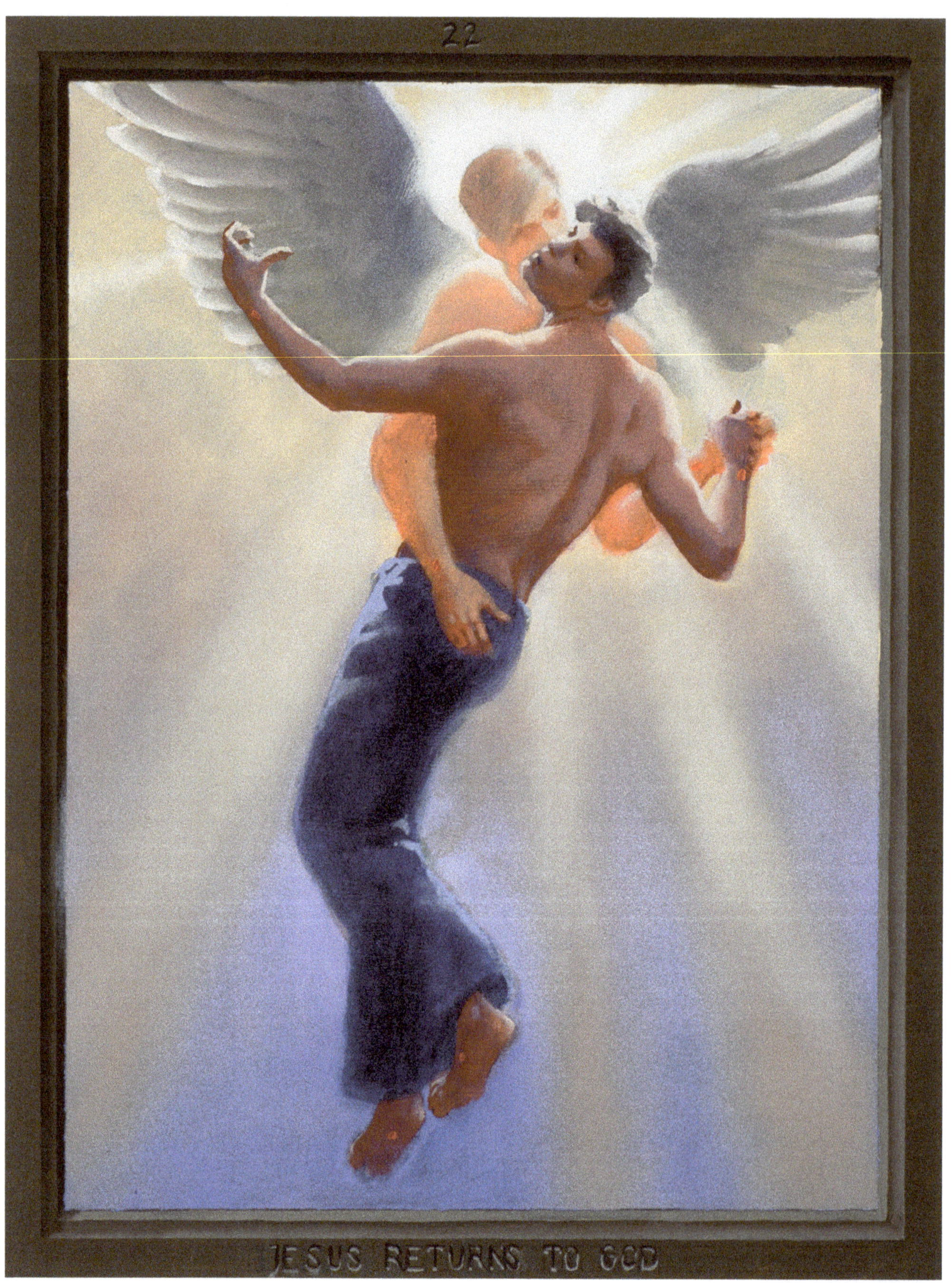

COLLECTION OF THE ARTIST

22. Jesus Returns to God

"O that you would kiss me with the kisses of your mouth!" —Song of Songs 1:2

Two young men dance skyward in the mystical homoerotic union of *Jesus Returns to God*. Jesus, shirtless and wearing blue jeans, swoons in the arms of a winged dance partner who appears to be a hunky male angel. But they both have crucifixion wounds on their wrists. Jesus is embraced directly by God! The position of their arms suggests a ballroom dance, perhaps a waltz, with God's hand planted firmly on Jesus' bottom.

Beams of white light stream from God's head in a bright sunburst, almost obliterating the blue sky. His wings look muscular, as if God must work hard to lift the dead weight of Jesus up from the earth. The wounds in Jesus' wrists and feet were dark before, but now they glow like hot-pink jewels. Dissolving into white at the top, this is the lightest painting in Blanchard's Passion series, contrasting with the pitch-black panel of *Jesus Among the Dead*. Now the misty clouds even spill over the frame on the lower left. The Bible and creeds make it clear where the dancing couple is headed. Soon Jesus will sit at the right hand of God.

Jesus Returns to God provides a gay vision of the Ascension, the transitional moment when the resurrected Christ left earth. Details vary, but all Biblical accounts agree that Jesus was with his followers when he was lifted up to heaven. Churches commemorate the event with the Feast of the Ascension forty days after Easter. Christian tradition emphasizes that the resurrected Jesus rose bodily up into the clouds of heaven. Mortal human flesh was made radiant by becoming part of God. Therefore it is appropriate for this image to have a physical, erotic component, even though some viewers find it disturbing.

People tend to react strongly to this image. Some find it too sexual and recoil at the thought of "God's hand on my butt." (At least God has no body below the waist here!) Others welcome the painting because it removes the shame of sexuality, presenting erotic love as holy. Sacred same-sex kisses are rarer in art than gay bashings, so the most daring part of Blanchard's Passion series occurs here after Jesus dies. Holy gay kisses also upset most people more than two men attacking each other. With this image Blanchard's series truly becomes a "gay vision" as the title proclaims. There is no longer any doubt about whether Jesus was simply an ally of queer people. The full revelation of his gay sexual orientation does not happen in his lifetime, but is disclosed in the afterlife by Blanchard. Some people wish the series stopped right before this image. Others would prefer it started here.

Blanchard breaks new ground by combining the Ascension with the Christian concept of "mystical marriage" from a gay viewpoint, making this one of the most original paintings in the series. In Christian theology the Ascension serves to emphasize the reality of Jesus as both human and divine. It is seen as the consummation of God's union with humanity. "Mystical marriage" is a separate Christian concept in which the love between God and people is compared to a human marriage, including the sexual ecstasy between bride and groom. Erotic union becomes a metaphor for union with God. This understanding dates back at least as far as Solomon's Song of Songs in the Hebrew Scriptures.

God appears here for the first time in Blanchard's Passion series. The artist paints God with some extraordinary attributes: He has wings, wounds, and the same face as Jesus. It is unusual to see a painting of God with wings, even though there are several Biblical references to humanity being protected or carried by God's wings. The wings here might symbolize the presence of the Holy Spirit. Standard images show God and Jesus as father and son, but Blanchard makes them look like gay lovers or the same person in two places, further emphasizing his theme of God in solidarity with humanity. Usually only Jesus has crucifixion wounds, but here the all-powerful creator is also a wounded deity, injured by choosing mortality in order to help people.

The mystical marriage and Christ the Bridegroom are uncommon subjects in art history, but the Ascension has been painted many times over the centuries. Ascension images generally have two zones: a crowd of apostles watching from earth below and Christ rising up toward heaven above. Jesus is frequently shown with his right hand raised in a gesture of blessing. Sometimes just his feet are visible as he disappears into the clouds. Artists seldom depict only Jesus and God without the people below, as Blanchard does. A notable exception is the famed *Ascension* by 20th-century surrealist Salvador Dali, which is dominated by the soles of Jesus' feet as he flies upward.

While it fits neatly into the Passion series, *Jesus Returns to God* can also stand alone as a gay-affirming vision of ecstatic union with God. The mixed response to the painting raises questions about how artists can visually code Jesus as queer without being too literal. Conservative Christians have made many LGBT people think of Jesus as their enemy. How far should an artist go to counteract that? For some viewers, anything more than a subtle hint is too sexually explicit or reduces the mystery of Christ to a billboard. Others need a boldly out-and-proud Jesus to prove that God loves LGBT folk. Blanchard strikes a balance by showing Jesus as an ordinary man swept up in a homoerotic dance with God. ●

"As the bridegroom rejoices over the bride,

so shall your God rejoice over you." —Isaiah 62:5

Surely Jesus felt bliss when he returned to God. Some compare the joy of a soul's union with the divine to sexual ecstasy in marriage. Perhaps for Jesus, it was a same-sex marriage. Jesus drank in the nectar of God's breath and surrendered to the divine embrace. They mixed male and female in ineffable ways. Jesus became both Lover and Beloved as everything in him found in God its complement, its reflection, its twin. When they kissed, Jesus let holy love flow through him to bless all beings throughout timeless time. Love and faith touched; justice and peace kissed. The boundaries between Jesus and God disappeared and they became whole: one Heart, one Breath, One. We are all part of Christ's body in a wedding that welcomes everyone.

Jesus, congratulations on your wedding day!
Thank you for inviting me!

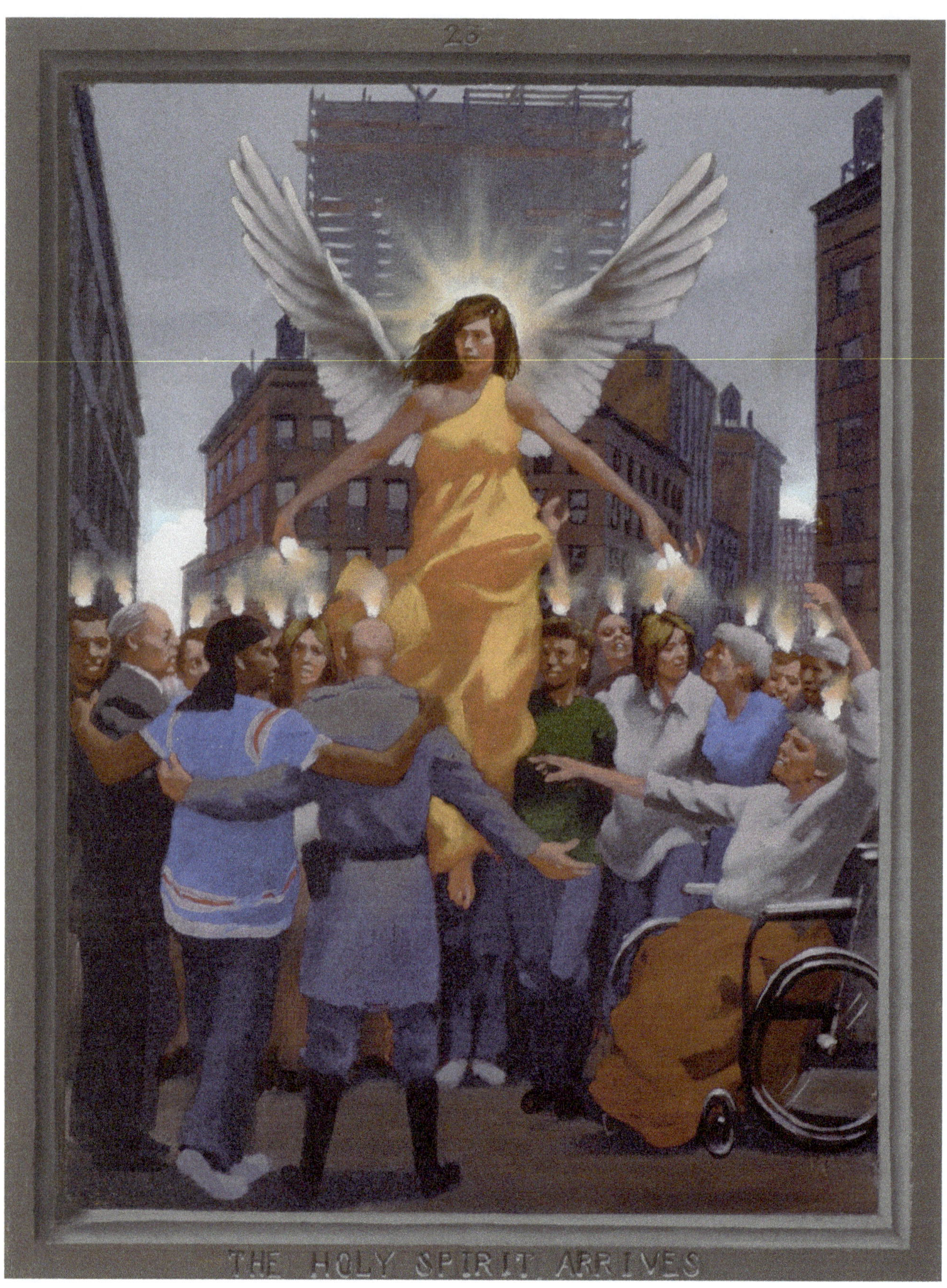

PRIVATE COLLECTION

23. The Holy Spirit Arrives

"There appeared to them tongues as of fire, distributed and resting on each one of them. And they were all filled with the Holy Spirit." —Acts 2:3-4

A winged woman literally lights up a crowd in *The Holy Spirit Arrives*. Carrying flares in both hands, she ignites tiny flames that blaze on the heads of the people. The Holy Spirit floats like an angel above an intersection where darkened city streets meet at odd angles. The dusky sky and unlit buildings strike a mysterious mood, making miracles possible. The group joins arms, forming a circle. Filled with the spirit, they make strange alliances. A soldier, a gang-banger, and a businessman wrap their arms around each other. An older woman and a younger woman embrace. The person in the wheelchair appears to be the same hothead who demanded the death of Christ in *Jesus Before the People*. Nobody is left cold. Looming behind them is a large building under construction. The painting is a modern version of Pentecost, when the Holy Spirit came to Jesus' disciples like tongues of fire and inspired them to speak in other languages.

The Holy Spirit Arrives gives visual form to a moment of spiritual transcendence. It is the only painting in Blanchard's Passion series that does not show Jesus. And yet Jesus *is* present within the people. They have been transformed by the Holy Spirit into the body of Christ. Everyone is enflamed—not just the twelve apostles. Christ has multiple manifestations both inside and outside the church in today's pluralistic society. The painting also hints that Jesus is present in the form of the Holy Spirit. They both have the same face. This, Blanchard says, is deliberate. By making Jesus and the Holy Spirit look alike, he emphasizes that they are one being. Christ, who is both male and female, can easily change genders.

"I will pour out my Spirit upon all flesh." —Joel 2:28

Jesus promised his friends that the Holy Spirit would come to empower them. They were together in the city on Pentecost when suddenly they heard a strong windstorm blowing in the sky. Tongues of fire appeared and separated to land on each one of them. Jesus' friends were flaming, on fire with the Holy Spirit! Soon the Spirit led them to speak in other languages. The commotion drew a big crowd. Good people from every race and nation came from all over the city. They brought their beautiful selves like the colors of the rainbow. Each one was able to hear about God in his or her own language. Inspired by the Holy Spirit, we too can hear and speak God's story. We are the flaming friends of Christ!

Come, Holy Spirit, and kindle a flame of love in my heart.

The story of Pentecost is told in Acts 2 of the Bible. The apostles were sitting together indoors early one morning when they heard wind rushing. Tongues of fire landed on each of them. Inspired by the Spirit, they spoke in other tongues and a crowd gathered. Devout people from all over the world were amazed to hear the mighty works of God in their own languages. But some scoffed, so Peter explained by quoting a prophecy from the Book of Joel: "I will pour out my Spirit upon all flesh, and your sons and your daughters shall prophesy, and the young shall see visions, and the old shall dream dreams." (Acts 2:17*) Jesus himself predicted that the Holy Spirit would come after him to empower his disciples to do "even greater things" than he did. The word rendered as "Spirit" can also mean wind, breath, advocate, comforter, or teacher.

Earlier in the Passion series the crowd strained to touch Christ or follow his lead, but now they have absorbed his teachings and indeed his spirit. The transformation of the crowd on Pentecost becomes more visible when contrasted with the masses who marched with Jesus on Palm Sunday. Blanchard's second painting and the second-to-last paintings are paired, just like the first and last. In the past the crowd marched into the city carrying signs, but they didn't look at each other. Now they have no need for placards or slogans. Turning to each other, they find among themselves the freedom and justice that they had sought to gain. They have been tested in ways that were unimaginable on Palm Sunday and forged into true community. They experience God effortlessly, involuntarily. Despite their otherworldly flames, they are more present in the world than they were before. The Palm Sunday setting was sterile and empty except for the triumphal arch, but this crowd gathers on a realistic city street where people actually live.

The Biblical idea of a fire burning on one's head is scary as well as implausible, but the flames brought by Blanchard's Holy Spirit look friendly and tame, like birthday candles. Sometimes Pentecost is called the birthday of the church. Like the burning bush of Moses, the holy fire doesn't consume. The building under construction in the background can be interpreted as the foundation of the Christian church. The artist himself offered an alternative view: "I prefer to think of it as a reference to the story of the Tower of Babel." The Book of Genesis says that the Tower of Babel was going to be tall enough to reach heaven, but God interrupted the building process by creating multiple languages, thus halting communication. The action was reversed at Pentecost, when the Holy Spirit removed language barriers. The early church taught that the arrival of the Holy Spirit reopened paradise, which had been closed by human sin.

Many of the previous paintings have a tight, sometimes claustrophobic focus. Blanchard's Pentecost comes like a breath of fresh air that shows the big picture at last. The past comes into perspective and the viewer can see the neighborhood where Jesus lived and died. The artist says that he did not intend any particular location. Intersections like this are common in New York City. One of the many places it resembles is the site of the 1911 Triangle Shirtwaist Factory fire where 146 garment workers died, the deadliest industrial disaster in New York history. That destructive fire contrasts with the transformative flames of the Spirit.

Blanchard takes Pentecost out into the

streets and humanizes it by presenting the Holy Spirit as a woman. In church texts the Holy Spirit is sometimes described as the female person of the Trinity. She is known as Sophia, the embodiment of Wisdom. But at other times She is referred to as "He," a rather queer blurring of gender duality. Blanchard's bold female Holy Spirit is one of the most unusual features of this painting from an art historical perspective. Artists generally depict the Holy Spirit at Pentecost as a descending dove, not as a woman. Blanchard gives her the wings of a dove. The contour of the building behind the Holy Spirit also looks like a dove, mirroring the shape in the background of *Jesus Appears to His Friends.* Paintings of Pentecost are often called "The Descent of the Holy Spirit," but Blanchard removes the top-down implications by titling it *The Holy Spirit Arrives.*

Viewers may be surprised to find Pentecost in a series on the Passion of Christ. Artists do not always conclude the Passion narrative with Jesus' death, resurrection, or even his ascension. Blanchard acknowledges that one of the inspirations for this series is Albrecht Dürer's Small Passion. He follows Dürer's example by continuing the Passion for two more panels after the Ascension. Both artists portray Pentecost as the next-to-last image. In Blanchard's gay Passion, Pentecost is a stopping point near the end of the road from prison to paradise.

Christians today believe that the Holy Spirit continues to be active, especially in times of trouble or celebration. Progressive Christians recognize the work of the Spirit when churches begin to embrace LGBT members, bless same-sex marriages, ordain openly LGBT clergy, and teach queer theology. In light of Pentecost, it may be significant that the most outrageously effeminate gay men have been disparaged as "flaming." The bundles of sticks used to burn heretics were called "faggots," now an insult for gay men.

The Pentecost story is good news for LGBT people because the Holy Spirit comes to *all* people, regardless of sexual orientation or gender identity. The Spirit ignites the desire to be true to oneself, even when that means being fully, flagrantly queer. LGBT people can identify with the Holy Spirit's combustible mix of male and female. The Holy Spirit, whose own gender is ambiguous, welcomes those who are called bulldykes or fairies, amazons or eunuchs, transfolk or genderqueer, two-spirit or third-gender. Every language has words for queer people, and the story of Jesus has been translated into many languages. Thanks to the multilingual marvels of Pentecost, the gospel is now available with a gay accent. ●

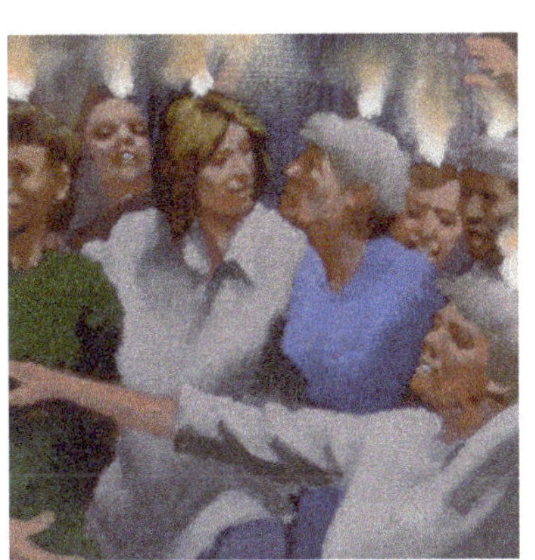

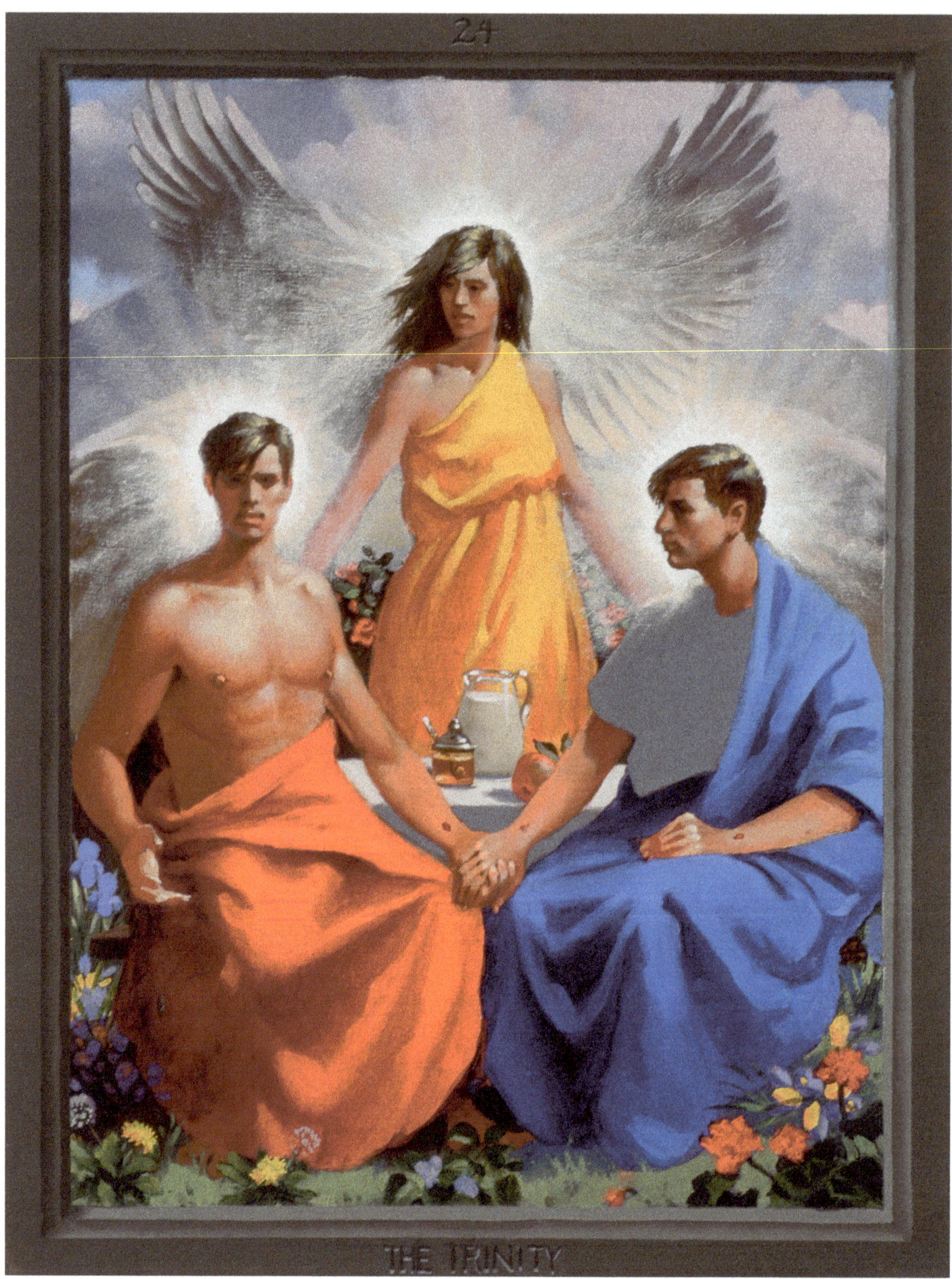

COLLECTION OF THE ARTIST

24. The Trinity

"Blessed are those who are persecuted for righteousness' sake, for theirs is the realm of heaven." —Matthew 5:10*

An angelic figure blesses a gay couple in *The Trinity*, the final, climactic image in Blanchard's Passion of Christ. They hold hands before a table set with milk, honey, and fruit—references to the Promised Land. The man draped in red reaches out, coaxing the viewer to join them in the sunny garden. The winged woman in the golden robe is the same Holy Spirit who arrived in the previous painting. An arch in the background hints at the gate of heaven. Viewers are welcome to imagine themselves seated in paradise with Christ as their bridegroom.

The Trinity shows how Jesus has been transformed by his experience of the Passion. He moved from the dark prison of the first painting to a bright land of promise, out of the closet, into the streets, and on to holy bliss. He completed the mythic hero's journey: martyred and reborn with power to redeem the world. The painting can stand alone to affirm the goodness of same-sex couples, but it also serves as a foretaste of paradise and a meditation on the Christian Trinity: one God in three persons. The whole concept of a three-in-one God with male and female aspects is rather queer because it means that God does not fit the standard gender binary, but may be transgender, omnigender, or genderqueer. A lot of LGBT people and allies just plain like *The Trinity*, without seeing it as Christian at all. It was chosen to illustrate the concept of gay friendship on the cover of *White Crane Journal: Gay Wisdom and Culture* in summer 2007. The artist has said that he intended this image to be "a little glimpse of salvation, of the reward of the faithful."

Viewers will be forgiven for wondering which man is Jesus. Blanchard, who is so adept at painting individual faces, gives the same face to all three, even the female Holy Spirit.

The artist said he did this on purpose to emphasize the three-in-one nature of God. The Trinity concept is reinforced by the colors of their clothing. The red, blue, and yellow robes are the three primary colors that, when mixed, create the full spectrum of white light. Red, yellow, and blue flowers blossom around them. These are common garden-variety plants: irises, geraniums—and dandelions! Even weeds are welcome at the feet of Christ. Blanchard's heaven is not a faraway, immaterial afterlife, but an earthly garden in this present paradise. The natural setting and robes give it a timeless quality, but there are hints of contemporary life in the glass pitcher and honey jar. The man on the right wears a modern T-shirt under his blue robe.

One clue to their identities comes from the way the figures direct their attention. The Holy Spirit and the man in blue focus on the man in red. Their body language suggests that he is Jesus, the center of this series, the one who just completed his heroic Passion journey. Like Christ in Blanchard's first painting, the man in red gazes straight ahead, meeting the eyes of the viewer. His upper torso is naked, revealing the wound in his side and a radiant, muscular body. Surely this is Jesus.

God and Jesus are shown as identical young lovers in a mystic same-sex marriage.

The Bible says that Jesus will ascend to heaven and sit at the right hand of God. By that reckoning, the man in blue must be God, but he is not the usual Father figure of traditional Trinitarian imagery. He doesn't look like "the Lord" and is certainly not old enough to be Jesus' father. In Blanchard's universe, God's identification with humanity is so complete that God and Jesus are identical young lovers in a mystic same-sex marriage, both sharing the same crucifixion wounds. Mission accomplished, they sit together side by side in radical equality. As the historical Christian creeds say, they are "of one substance" and "coeternal and coequal."

The holy gay wedding imagery is especially revolutionary because of its placement in Blanchard's Passion sequence. After the Ascension and Pentecost, the final position in a Passion cycle normally goes to the Last Judgment. Traditional images show Jesus condemning sinners to hell and sending the righteous to heaven. Conservative Christians like to imagine homosexuals among the damned. But Blanchard rejects the crime-based model. Jesus and God are not on thrones nor do they judge anybody. Indeed, Blanchard reverses the whole Christian view of history as presented by countless artists, including his acknowledged inspiration, Albrecht Dürer. In his 16th-century Small Passion, Dürer began with Adam and Eve eating for-

"Truly, I say to you, today you will be with me in Paradise."— Luke 23:43

Look, the Holy Spirit celebrates two men who love each other! She looks like an angel as She protects the male couple. Are the men Jesus and God? No names can fully express the omnigendered Trinity of Love, Lover, and Beloved… or Mind, Body, and Spirit. God is madly in love with everybody. God promises to lead people out of injustice and into a good land flowing with milk and honey. We can travel along the same path to paradise where Jesus journeyed. Opening to the joy and pain of the world, we can experience all of creation as our body—the body of Christ. As queer as it sounds, we can create our own land of milk and honey. As Jesus often said, heaven is among us and within us. Now that we have seen a gay vision of Christ's Passion, we are free to move forward with passion.

Jesus, thank you for giving me a new vision!

Blanchard's Passion concludes
not with judgment,
but with love
as its crowning glory.

bidden fruit and being expelled from Eden as punishment. He ended with the Last Judgment. By contrast Blanchard starts with punishment in prison, and then finds a way to paradise. He chose a prototype for this painting in a separate branch of art history: Andrei Rublev's great Byzantine icon *Trinity,* which shows the three angels at Abraham's table.

Blanchard's Passion concludes not with judgment, but with love as its crowning glory. Most artists throughout history have not used couples to symbolize the joys of heaven, but some contemporary LGBT artists do. Both Blanchard and Swedish photographer Elisabeth Ohlson Wallin envision same-sex pairs in the afterlife. Ohlson Wallin closes her *Ecce Homo* series with a vision of heaven in which Jesus and his boyfriend are surrounded by a crowd of loving lesbian and gay couples, all clad in white.

The painting that ends the gay Passion has a lot in common with the first painting, which shows Jesus as the Human One / Son of Man with Job and Isaiah. The opening picture also forms a kind of Trinity. Unlike the rest of the series, their titles are theological concepts. Both have interrupted the flow of time, mixing modern and pre-Christian dress. Both show Jesus gazing directly into the eyes of the viewer. The first and last images are like brackets that enclose and uphold the events in Christ's life.

After moving through the whole Passion series, viewers have witnessed God's solidarity with humankind and seen the power of love to transcend personal suffering, human history, and even death itself. They have encountered Jesus, the wounded healer, the hated lover, the crucified creator, the liberator in chains, the all-too-human child of God. The gay vision of Christ's Passion leaves viewers with an invitation to rise up and love as Jesus does. The painting ends the series as a visual benediction, encouraging viewers to carry the vision onward and live with passion. ●

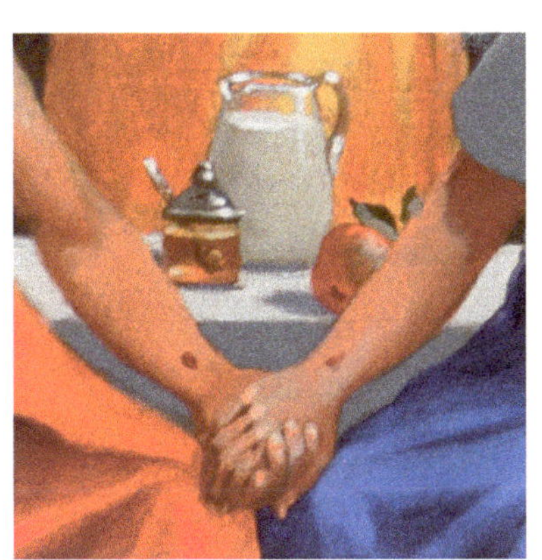

Afterword: The Passion of the Christ through New Eyes

BY TOBY JOHNSON

Something new is happening. Religion and spirituality are undergoing a radical transformation. Gay consciousness and the suffering of queer and deviant people is part of the transformation. Our eyes are being opened to a higher understanding. The way people today understand religious meaning is changing. Because we know about all the gods and all the religions, we are forced to rise to a perspective that can include them all. Because we know about homosexuality and sexual variation, we are forced to reach a broader perspective on what it means to be human and embodied. We are forced to see through new eyes.

In the comparative religions model, all the religions are true when understood from an outsider perspective. Gay people are naturals for such an understanding. As we learn to include our sexual difference in our self-concepts, we almost necessarily, even automatically, learn to see from a different perspective—if nothing else, one that at least includes homosexuality. We learn to see the world that other people take for granted with different eyes. I think this is a queer talent that many of us learn, similar to fashion design, floral arrangement, hair styling, artistry, acting, etc. It's why so many of us have been priests, and why so many have been heretics.

An enlightened perspective on religious stories shows that they are not really about the historical or trans-historical characters, in real time or in sacred time, but rather that the story is about *you*. The message of all the religions is how *you* can live a rich, rewarding, participating, contributing, meaningful life. *You* are the main character of every story. What an enlightenment!

In that vein, with a certain enlightened perspective, oil painter Douglas Blanchard portrays Jesus in this book as a modern gay man in modern clothing. He is cheered by his friends, but then brutalized by police and by fag-baiting protestors. The disturbing, but ultimately glorious, series of twenty-four paintings forces the viewer to consider that anti-gay violence in the name of religion is an exact parallel to the violence done against Jesus and which Christians believe was salvific for us all. If suffering is salvific, then gay people are world saviors, too. The paintings ask us to reconsider what saving the world means, and how, for us at least, same-sex love fits integrally into the vision.

Using a similar perspective, art historian and internet activist Kittredge Cherry provides an introduction and heartfelt, inspiring commentary for each painting—all pointing toward that transformed vision. This book is the most recent of many projects in which she presents a gay Jesus—over angry objections from conservatives. They seem to see only the Jesus of history and fail to see the Christ that lives in all of us. Cherry is the author of the remarkable *Jesus in Love*, a life of Christ titled with obvious allusion to D.H. Lawrence and the literature of acknowledged sexuality. She does what few writers have ever dared: to acknowledge that Jesus was a sexual human being. Cherry manages a website that features religious, erotic/homoerotic art. That too certainly angers traditionalists. With our queer eyes, we're able to see that these qualities are perfectly compatible—and that's a new thing too. Kitt seems to attract controversy, and the controversy over gay and lesbian—queer—sexualities is one of the cultural factors driving the transformation of religion. So I am proud of Kitt and Doug for stirring things up.

The Passion isn't just about Jesus in Jerusalem two thousand years ago, but about the Christ that is in all of us and of which all of us are constituent parts. That's the meaning of placing the Passion in modern times and Jesus in a modern—even a gay man's—body. The Stations of the Cross are happening now. We contemplate these stories, not just to feel compunction or guilt or self-satisfied righteousness for Jesus' sake, but to call ourselves to stop the suffering. Now is the time we save the world. These stories change us by sensitizing us and motivating us to wake up.

Christ, after all, transcends Jesus, the man of history. Christ is the Greek word, meaning "anointed," that was used to translate *Messiah*; it's the same word in the name of the Hindu incarnated god Krishna. It's a title given to Jesus identifying his role as world savior. In its richest sense, it refers to The Mystical Body of Christ—the collective being of Earth made up of all human souls with Jesus as the exemplar and archetype—experiencing life here and now as the Kingdom of Heaven.

The problem of suffering is real. Jesus, in us as us, is being tortured today—in the Middle East, in terrorist attacks, in prisons and gulags, and in government-approved oppression of the poor and the unfortunate and the queer and sexually different. It is the Mystical Body of Christ that is under attack—and, tragically, sometimes from those who call themselves followers of Jesus.

Like many people, I have great affection for Christian tradition, but I have a problem with the theology that developed to explain "why Christ had to suffer and die." The emphasis on the specifics of Jesus' death and the notion that life is a vale of tears shifted the focus of Christianity toward achieving afterlife and shunning the real world of human experience. What Kitt and Doug are doing is radically transforming the mythology that has been erected around the Passion.

In some ways, I still think of myself as a devout Catholic—just a little betrayed by the Church. I don't have much resonance with all that stuff about original sin at the dawn of time and Jesus as a blood sacrifice to the Father's wrath in order to save humans from the fires of Hell after death and get them into an ethereal Heaven. What needs saving is the world here and now, and Jesus' message of love is the mechanism for saving it.

I remember as a child in Catholic school being horrified and intimidated by the teaching that every time we committed a sin we drove the nail deeper into Jesus' hand. You know, if that "sin" had been murder and mayhem then maybe that scary lesson would have been appropriate. But to six-year-olds for whom "sin" meant "disobeying my parents three times and fighting with my brother once," driving nails through somebody's hand is just too much... And later that image got applied to innocent sexual experimentation—and to homosexual feelings. Tragically, Christianity is sometimes the medium by which such life-destructive values are conditioned into people, resulting in terrible wars, genocides of native people, and denial of modern realities.

That is *not*, of course, to question the *teachings* of Jesus. But it's the mythology that arose around him—counter to most everything he is said to have taught—that has created the problems. Jesus was murdered by the religious authorities for preaching that love and compassion are more important than rules. That is a message that still makes sense to us today. Jesus died for integrity and truth—not to appease an angry God. We need to reassess what all that blood was about in Christian history. But the really interesting issue isn't judging Christianity or any mythological system; it's seeing now how they are all being changed by modern, global consciousness.

Renowned comparative religions scholar and mythographer Joseph Campbell was the Great Teacher and "Wise Old Man" of my personal spiritual journey. From him I learned that all religions represent different interpretations of the vast, elusive truth about life itself. It's like the parable of the Five Blind Men and the Elephant: in order to discover the elephant, you have to combine all five perspectives, all five senses, then achieve a mental insight into what kind of larger truth could include them all. Today's trans-historical, psychologically sophisticated perspective offers a higher, more expansive, more inclusive way of understanding religious meaning. The truth in the religions is metaphorical more than historical. The truth of a religious doctrine is measured in the positive, transformational power it holds for believers.

Jesus is a symbol in story and myth for the Self in every person. That's why Jesus can be painted as Black or Asian or American-Indian, as Jewish or white European, as man or woman, as ancient or modern, as gay or straight. Jesus is Everyman. And every man and woman—and every possible variation—can be seen as Jesus: "Whatsoever you do to the least of these, that you do to me." Our comparative religions model allows us to see that every one of us human beings is savior of his or her own life; we all suffer and we all strive to transcend and go on.

Christ crucified is human consciousness stretched out in the four directions of the compass and affixed, nailed, to physical manifestation by the five senses that are symbolized by the five wounds in Jesus' hands, feet, head, and heart. Jesus' death represents an acceptance of the realities of human existence. I think we're supposed to see that Jesus says "yes" to life—no matter what the content or appearance of that life is. So he says "yes" even to crucifixion and death.

In the interviews still occasionally shown on PBS as *The Power of Myth*, Joseph Campbell comments: "People ask me, 'Do you have optimism about the world?' And I say, 'Yes, it's great just the way it is.'" That's the nature of life. It wouldn't be life if it weren't like that. You have to say "yes" to it. Journalist Bill Moyers asks: "Doesn't that lead to a rather passive attitude in the face of evil?" Campbell insists that, oh no, it doesn't mean that at all: "You yourself are participating in the evil, or you are not alive."

For part of "the way it is" is that you want to change things, that you're indignant about injustice and unnecessary suffering, that you are motivated to seek change. Saying "yes" to life is saying "yes" to the whole work of making this a better world, and especially a world motivated by compassion. Ironically, resisting the way things are by judging and condemning just keeps them going, because then this world looks like a vale of tears, and that's what it remains. Accepting and embracing things as they are allows you to see the Kingdom of God, heaven here and now, because heaven is how it will become when everybody stops resisting and judging, allows compassion and caring to guide them, and everybody says "yes" to life.

Jesus says "yes" to life, no matter what the content or appearance.

The message is to affirm life, to experience eternity here and now, no matter what it seems to look like. "This is it. And if you don't get it here, you won't get it anywhere," Campbell said. His spirituality is appropriately called, "The Way of Joyful Participation in the Sorrows of the World."

That's the phrase Campbell uses for the myth of the world savior who also says "yes" in Mahayana Buddhism. He told Moyers, "The Buddhists speak of bodhisattva—the one who knows immortality, yet voluntarily enters into the field of fragmentation of time and participates willingly and joyfully in the sorrows of the world. And this means not only experiencing sorrows oneself but participating with compassion in the sorrow of others."

In Mahayana Buddhism one important bodhisattva is called Avalokiteshvara—the name means "The Enlightened Being Who Looks Down with Compassion." This bodhisattva is more a character

Embracing and understanding suffering releases us from suffering.

of myth and story than history, living in sacred time, not real time. Avalokiteshvara is androgynous, including both male and female. He is sometimes portrayed as a lovable young man sitting in a relaxed meditation pose; sometimes portrayed as a woman, the Goddess of Compassion, Kuan Yin.

Avalokiteshvara was about to enter nirvana, a state beyond life and death, and leave behind forever the world of suffering when he/she heard a groan go up from nature; it was the suffering of all sentient beings. The young Buddhist saint had a profound pang of compassion for other beings. Realizing it would be better for one to suffer than for all, he/she asked to take on the suffering of all sentient beings. He/she made a vow to delay his/her own entry into nirvana until all other beings could enter nirvana and, indeed, to let all others go first by assuming all their future reincarnations for them, so that he/she is the only Being living out all our lives, suffering our pain and sufferings. We are all incarnations of Avalokiteshvara—the name can also be interpreted to mean "The Lord Who Is Seen Within." This is why we should feel compassion for others: they are us, too.

I learned the story from reading Campbell's *The Hero with a Thousand Faces* when I was in college in the late 1960s. I remember recognizing vividly that Avalokiteshvara's decision was the right one, the one I would have wanted to make. Is that because I'm a reincarnation of Avalokiteshvara? Well, of course; that's the myth. But I think also it was because as a sensitive gay youth, I felt naturally obligated to compassion and generosity. This was self-sacrifice, not for shame and compulsion, but for "apotheosis"—that's the name of the chapter in Campbell's book about the bodhisattva—"becoming God."

All Mahayana Buddhists are urged to repeat the Bodhisattva Vows daily, not only as a reminder to themselves of who they really are in their deepest selves, but also to remind them to be compassionate and generous. If we're all compassionate and generous, most of the suffering in the world *will* go away. Embracing and understanding suffering releases us from suffering. Underlying all Buddhist teachings is the notion that the real suffering people experience is their resistance to what's happening. However terrible an event or situation, we can cope with it so much better if we aren't in denial and resistance. This is the basis of the healing power of psychotherapy as well.

In the Gnostic Acts of John, Jesus is said to have led the Apostles in a circle dance following the Last Supper in which he instructed them: "Learn how to suffer and you shall be able not to suffer." When I was reading *The Hero with a Thousand Faces*, there was a song on a Peter, Paul and Mary album composed by Richard and Mimi Fariña: "If somehow you could pack up your sorrows and give them all to me, you would lose them, I know how to use them. Give them all to me." That was about the bodhisattva myth. That is, in effect, the Bodhisattva Vow.

This myth was popularized by Buddhist sages around the same time that Jesus was living and teaching in Palestine. Some religion scholars believe the Buddhist myth may be based on the story of Jesus—or vice versa. (My own sense, by the way, is that both stories arose spontaneously within their respective cultures because of a profound shift in the collective consciousness. In a way not unlike the current shift in religion to understand myths as metaphors for consciousness, so around the beginning of the first millennium, the focus of religion shifted from obedience to rules and taboos to moral concern about other people. Both Jesus and Avalokiteshvara represent the maturation of religion into morality based in love of neighbor and compassion.)

In my view the Hindu/Buddhist afterlife model of reincarnation provides a more understandable and salutary mechanism of saving all beings than Jesus' appeasing the anger of a bloodthirsty God by becoming the ultimate scapegoat and final human sacrifice. But the mystical teaching of both stories is very much the same: the divine spark lives in each human being; salvation is found by seeing who you really are in this life, without judgment. It's about those transformed eyes again.

An icon of the bodhisattva in the form of a goddess named Tara shows her, like Jesus, with "wounds" in her hands, feet, head and heart; through Tara's wounds, eyes look out to see the world differently. We too are supposed to see through the wounds of Jesus with transformed and liberated eyes. Believing in Jesus is supposed to transform your life so that you do not suffer and do not cause suffering to others. Contemplating the Passion is supposed to transform you with compassion.

The "Stations of the Cross" in this book expand upon the *Via Dolorosa*, the Passion of the Catholic ritual. Blanchard's painting *Jesus Appears at Emmaus* demonstrates the recognition of Christ in everyone: the disciples did not see that the stranger they met on the road was Jesus until their eyes were transformed. And as an alternative to the conventional Christian idea that we will be saved from the vale of tears in a heaven after death, the final three images portray Jesus returning to God so that God, as the Holy Spirit, can arrive among human beings, opening our eyes to spiritual vision. *The Trinity* completes the cycle by revealing the identity of Love, Lover, and Beloved; Mind, Body, and Spirit; Past, Present, and Future—all in the eternal here and now, and metaphorized as the love of sames: Father, Son, and Holy Spirit—all the same.

The Stations of the Cross were an old-time Catholic ritual. When I was a boy in parochial school, Stations was a special event during

Lent that got us out of school early on Friday afternoons. We got to sing Gregorian chant. And there was incense.

One of my earliest memories of myself as a devout Catholic youth and budding spiritual seeker is of being deeply moved one Friday afternoon by the singing of the *Parce Domine*. It was a beautiful chant, and unlike any other Gregorian that we sang. The verse translates as "Spare your people, Lord; do not be angry with us forever." It is sung in a minor key and is repeated three times, each time at a higher pitch. I don't think I really knew what the words meant, but the chant was so plaintive, so forlorn, and in the context of the recitation of the stages of Jesus' sorrowful journey to the Cross, so moving, I began to weep.

I remember having to make an excuse when my buddies razzed me for crying like a girl. "The incense got in my eyes," I fibbed, "...must be allergic." But, no, I was a gay boy feeling deeply—as I was supposed to. I was being affected by the myth. The symbol of suffering changed me.

I certainly didn't know anything about bodhisattvas when I was eight or nine years old, but looking back I realize in some mythical way that the *Parce Domine* that day was that same groan that woke Avalokiteshvara out of his meditation.

So I invite you, the reader, to join Kitt Cherry, Doug Blanchard, and me in proclaiming these Stations. This time the reminder is that, especially perhaps as gay men and lesbians and transsexuals and queers—strange people with strange ways of seeing things—we participate in the suffering of humankind. We are moved by it to work that it not happen again: No more war, no more empire, no more torture—those are clearly the messages to get from contemplating the passion of Jesus. We are also invited, I think, to move beyond our own individual suffering and life problems by discovering that we humans are all in this together; with grace and compassion and loving acceptance, we transform our vision—see with new eyes—so that Paradise comes around about us again, so we can say "Yes, it's great just the way it is."

In the apocryphal Gospel of Thomas, Jesus declared, "The Kingdom of Heaven is spread out upon the Earth, and people do not see it."

Here it is. Here and now. No matter what it looks like. That's the message of the Passion. ●

Toby Johnson, Ph.D., is a Roman Catholic monk turned LGBT activist, psychotherapist and spiritual author. After leaving seminary, he earned a master's degree in comparative religion and a doctorate in counseling psychology from the California Institute of Integral Studies. While on staff at a Jungian retreat program, he befriended mythology scholar Joseph Campbell and came to regard himself as "an apostle of Campbell's vision to the gay community." Johnson has written such influential books as Gay Spirituality: The Role of Gay Identity in the Transformation of Human Consciousness. *His accomplishments include serving as a literary editor at Lethe Press and prior to that as editor/publisher of* White Crane: A Quarterly Journal of Gay Men's Spirituality.

Acknowledgements

Many people joined us on the journey to share the gay vision of Christ's Passion. This book arose through our individual lives, filtered and refined by interactions with the LGBTQ community. The creative process relies on unsung heroes who work behind the scenes to make sure that the art can be seen and the words can be read. We appreciate the loving support we received from friends and strangers who cared about the vision.

John Mabry, the versatile genius behind Apocryphile Press, took the risk of publishing a book so radical that mainstream Christian publishers wouldn't touch it. Messages of inclusive liberation get out in the world because of brave souls like him. He is ahead of his time, yet steeped in tradition: part high-tech wizard and part reincarnation of a Renaissance Pope. Brilliant at both the theoretical and practical, he has been a pillar of support for years, first publishing some of the Passion paintings in my previous book *Art That Dares*. His design for this book is sheer elegance.

Major momentum came from the two places that exhibited the original Passion paintings: The Leslie-Lohman Museum of Gay and Lesbian Art in New York City and JHS Gallery in Taos, New Mexico. Charles Leslie and Frederic "Fritz" Lohman created a space for queer artists by founding the museum where the Passion made its debut with guidance from Wayne Snellen. At JHS Gallery Jodi and Michael Simmons treated both of us extremely well, truly embodying the spirit of Christ who goes out of his way for others.

Toby Johnson's complete comprehension of the importance of the queer Christ helped bring the book into being. Over the years he was always there when needed, seeking not so much to be understood as to understand. When he wrote the Afterword, he put the Passion into a larger context and used his voice to give more people access to a queer vision that frees the spirit and thwarts right-wing bigotry. Michael Bronski also believed in the gay Passion project enough to shepherd it toward publication. Because this book comes from a marginalized position in society, the wisdom and understanding of such mentors is a life-and-death matter aesthetically and spiritually.

The book version of the Passion began to take form in 2011 when Kitt posted her commentaries with each individual painting at the Jesus in Love Blog during Lent. The gay Passion attracted a niche audience from around the world, like gathering needles from dozens of haystacks. The lively discussions that arose are essential to grassroots literary ventures like this one.

Trudie Barreras, Eric Hays-Strom and Lynn Jordan freely shared their resources on many levels. As long-time members of Metropolitan Community Church, they laid much of the groundwork for everything the LGBTQ movement has become. Trudie, herself a compassionate and talented artist, has been instrumental from the beginning in fostering our creative projects through Jesus in Love. Lynn (aka "Queen Mother") brings old-school gay culture into the 21st century in the best way possible as a founding member of MCC San Francisco. He is still nurturing new generations 43 years later. Eric's enthusiasm, education, and spiritual depth helped Kitt think through her ideas. They are the gold standard of queer Christianity, the rock upon which the church—and this book—are built.

This book is an outgrowth of the Internet and it was enriched and fertilized by online communication. Fellow bloggers who made extraordinary efforts to spread the word while Kitt was developing the text include June ("Grandmère Mimi") Butler, Jonathan ("Madpriest") Hagger, and Terence Weldon. A warm thank-you for comments, correspondence, prayers, and all-around assistance to CJ Barker, Danny Berry, Ann Fontaine, Jendi Reiter, Scott Sella, Andrew Craig Williams, and other readers of Jesus in Love too numerous to name. Faithful supporters whose generosity laid the foundation for this book include Judith Finlay, Scott Hankins, Paul Hartman, Barbara Marian, and Colin Smith.

When Doug painted the series, he originally dedicated it to the Reverend Barbara Cawthorne Crafton, an Episcopal priest who has shown him much kindness and hospitality down through the years, including through some rough patches of destitution many years ago.

Paintings need homes and artists need patrons, so we thank the collectors who own panels from the Passion: Paul Bridgewater, Bill Carpenter, Norman Fox, Vincent Palange (who donated his painting to the Leslie-Lohman Foundation in memory of Louis Prudenti), Brian Lathrop, Robert Wilder Nightingale, Jodi and Michael Simmons, Bruce Goerlich, and those anonymous angels whose identities remain a mystery.

As author and artist we want to take a moment to thank each other for cooperation on this book. We have much in common but also embody opposites of male and female, East Coast and West Coast, so our partnership is an unexpected accomplishment, far from a foregone conclusion.

Saving the best for last, we are grateful to our life partners for the love that carried us through this project: Michael Bradley made a life together with Doug because, as the blues song says, "This is a mean old world to live in all by yourself," and we weren't meant to be alone, or at least lonely. Audrey Lockwood lit up Kitt's life with an unstoppable love, unique vision, and purity of emotion that made her Passion journey possible and joyous. As Shakespeare put it, she teaches the torches to burn bright.

Thanks be to God for everyone who inspired us and brought out the best in us. ●

About the Author and Artist

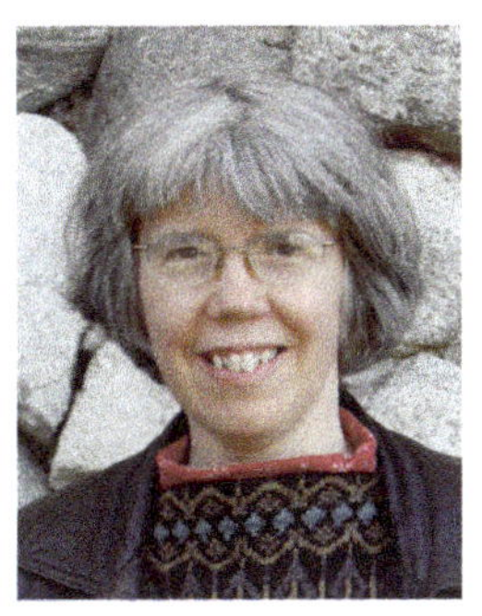

Author Kittredge Cherry is an art historian who founded Jesus in Love, an online resource for LGBT spirituality and the arts. Cherry was ordained by Metropolitan Community Churches and served as its National Ecumenical Officer, advocating for LGBT rights at the National Council of Churches and World Council of Churches. She holds degrees in journalism and art history from the University of Iowa, and a master of divinity degree from Pacific School of Religion. Her books include Lambda Literary Award finalist *Art That Dares: Gay Jesus, Woman Christ, and More* (AndroGyne Press), *Hide and Speak* (HarperSanFrancisco), *Womansword* (Kodansha International), and her *Jesus in Love* novels. *The New York Times Book Review* praised her "very graceful, erudite" writing style. Based in Los Angeles, she writes about LGBT spirituality and the arts at Huffington Post and the Jesus in Love Blog.

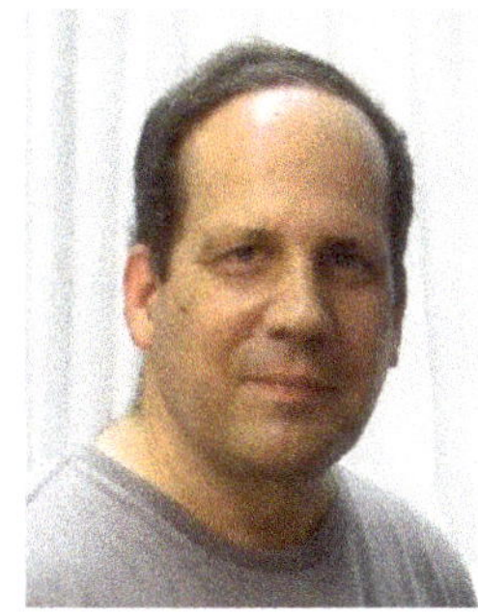

Artist Douglas Blanchard teaches art and art history at the Bronx Community College of the City University of New York. He paints in a realistic figurative style to explore gay experience as well as classical mythology, history, and current events. Born and raised in Dallas, Blanchard earned a BFA in painting from the Kansas City Art Institute in 1981, an MA in art history from Washington University in St. Louis in 1986, and an MFA cum laude from the New York Academy of Art in 1993. He was confirmed in the Episcopal Church in 1982 and remains an active Episcopalian and self-described "very agnostic believer." He keeps a studio on the Lower East Side of Manhattan. The Passion series was exhibited at New York's Leslie-Lohman Museum of Gay and Lesbian Art in 2004 and JHS Gallery in Taos, New Mexico in 2007. His other work has been shown at a variety of galleries, including the New York Academy of Art.

Comments from readers about
The Passion of Christ: A Gay Vision

"Accessible but profound!"
—Jean Gralley, artist/writer, Washington DC

"I just wish I had experienced this kind of queer-positive Christianity when I was a teen struggling with both my sexuality and my religion as a whole."
—Matt Leary, Dover, PA

"I can't go through Holy Week without recalling many of these images. They depict the Holy Week that is in my heart."
—Elisa Lucozzi, associate pastor, Saint Johnsbury, VT

"As a heretic Christian turned Buddhist, I was moved to tears by your artistic vision."
—John Gish

"I love these paintings not just for how 'radical' they are, but for how much I see them as being absolutely in line with traditional Christian understandings of Christ and of Easter."
—CJ Barker, activist, Marin County, CA

"The modern twist is disarming and, possibly, alarming but definitely something to contemplate."
—Benjamin Rexroad, artistic director, Akron, Ohio

If you enjoyed this book, please try Kittredge Cherry's other books:

ART THAT DARES: GAY JESUS, WOMAN CHRIST, AND MORE

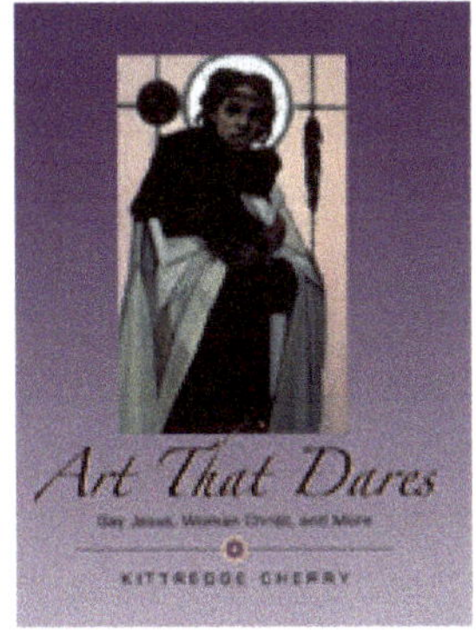

Art that Dares to show Jesus as gay or female has been censored or destroyed. Now for the first time these beautiful, liberating, sometimes shocking images are gathered for all to see. Packed with full-page color illustrations, this eye-opening collection features a diverse group of eleven contemporary artists who work both inside and outside the church. They present the gay Jesus, the woman Christ, and other cutting-edge Christian images. Their art respects the teachings of Jesus and frees the minds of viewers to see in new ways. Here the artists tell the stories behind their art. A lively introduction puts the images into political and historical context, exploring issues of blasphemy and artistic freedom.

"This...queer-eyed reworking of Christly iconography shows the power of re-imagining the traditionally sacred in light of the seemingly profane." —Michael Bronski, *The Guide*

"Her 'blasphemy' is so honest, so respectful, visionary, and inspiring that it becomes a kind of new religion...alive with imagery." —Toby Johnson, in *Lambda Book Report*

"Well written and beautifully illustrated."—Dignity USA *Quarterly Voice*

"Deftly compiled." —*Midwest Book Review*

"Suitable for coffee table and classroom." —Mary Hunt, *WATERwheel*

"I love this book. I celebrate the fact that once more Kittredge Cherry has moved beyond the flat, one-sided, predictable Jesus with blond hair and blue eyes to show us a living Christ who loved outcasts best and lived and died to prove it."
—Rev. Mel White, founder of Soulforce, LGBT Christian activist group

"*Art That Dares* is a stunning, artistically haunting, spiritually revolutionary, provocatively honest book that is a fresh alternative to deadened religiosity."
—The Rev. Canon Malcolm Boyd, poet, gay elder, author of *Are You Running with Me, Jesus?*

Lambda Literary Award finalist for Arts & Culture, 2007

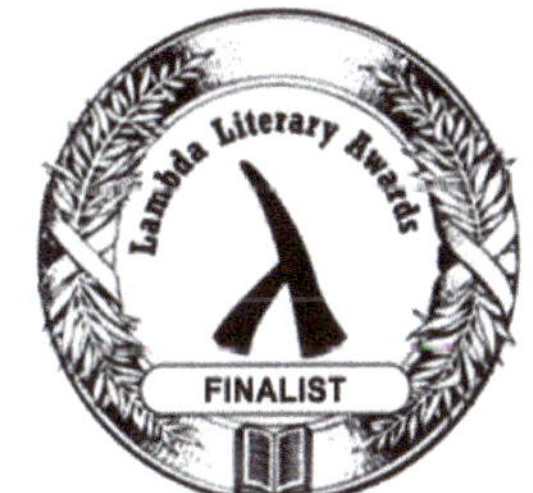

JESUS IN LOVE: A NOVEL

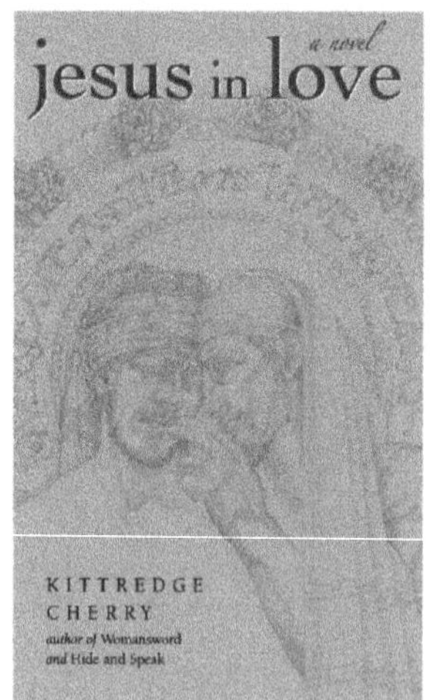

What if Jesus knew how it feels to be queer? Surprising answers come in *Jesus in Love*, a novel that re-imagines Christ's legendary life as an erotic, mystical adventure in first-century Palestine. Jesus has today's queer sensibilities and psychological sophistication as he lives out his mythic story. Readers can relate to the struggles he faces: He feels like his real self is both male and female. He falls in love with people of both sexes. Society doesn't understand him. Jesus, the narrator, speaks in an engaging, up-to-date tone as he reveals his intimate relationships with John the beloved disciple (a gay man mourning his lover's death), Mary Magdalene (a highly intelligent survivor of sexual abuse) and the multi-gendered Holy Spirit. The novel shows how Jesus grows over a one-year period-from his decision to get baptized until the day he sends his friends away to teach others. Ultimately he leads disciples of both sexes to a place where sexuality and spirituality are one. *Jesus in Love* frees the reader to imagine and experience Christ in new ways.

"In imagining a Jesus who really lived, laughed and loved, Kitt Cherry has broken through the stained glass barrier. Don't be afraid. This is not a prurient look at the sex life of Jesus but a classic re-telling of the greatest story ever told, the story of a truly human Jesus and those truly human women and men who lived, laughed and loved with him. Read *Jesus in Love* and you will feel His Spirit reaching out to you, inviting you to live, laugh and love with him as well."

—Rev. Mel White, founder of Soulforce and author of
Religion Gone Bad: The Hidden Dangers of the Christian Right

"A truly mind-blowing creation. The writing style is just perfect. *Jesus in Love* is a wonderful, gay-sensitive, and delightfully 'shocking' reassessment of the stories of the old-time religion. I promise you, you'll be surprised by the book."

—Toby Johnson, author of *Gay Spirituality* and former editor of
White Crane: A Journal of Gay Spirit

"What a lovely, gentle, playful book! It sparkles with erotic christic power, which we might read as an image of Jesus' own sexual energies. Kitt Cherry continues to write with passion as she draws creatively and faithfully from deep wellsprings of imagination."

—Rev. Carter Heyward, Ph.D., Howard Chandler Robbins
Professor Emerita of Theology, Cambridge, MA

"A book whose time has come. Many people will misunderstand this book—especially those who refuse to read it. It is a contemporary and creative work of fiction rooted in a sensibility of the search for holiness."

—Rev. Malcolm Boyd, author of *Are You Running with Me, Jesus?*

JESUS IN LOVE: AT THE CROSS
A SEQUEL TO JESUS IN LOVE

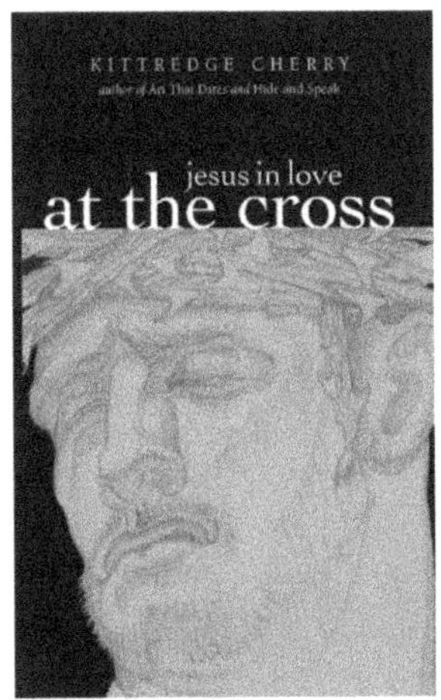

Picking up where *Jesus in Love* leaves off, *Jesus in Love: At the Cross* continues the story of Jesus' erotic, mystical adventures in first-century Palestine, this time all the way to his untimely death, his miraculous resurrection, and beyond. Jesus has today's queer sensibilities and psychological sophistication as he lives out his mythic story.

"Fearlessly enough Rev. Kittredge Cherry, the lesbian author known for her spellbinding homo-friendly Christian novels...defies all odds again continuing from her prequel *Jesus In Love*, with her latest *Jesus in Love: At the Cross*. In this novel Cherry explores the question of, 'What if Jesus were queer?' A risky and difficult approach, nonetheless, beautifully executed.... This book will stun the conservative religious reader. Regardless of sexual orientation or religion, this book is a good read for any open-minded reader."

—*Curve Magazine*, 2009

"A powerful celebration of Jesus' message of love." —*Tikkun Magazine*, July/August 2009

"A *real tour de force* in transforming traditional myth to modern consciousness."

—Toby Johnson, author of *Gay Spirituality*

"A daring and challenging portrait of an omnigendered, sensuous Christianity."

—Virginia Ramey Mollenkott, Ph.D., author of *Omnigender*

HIDE AND SPEAK: A COMING OUT GUIDE

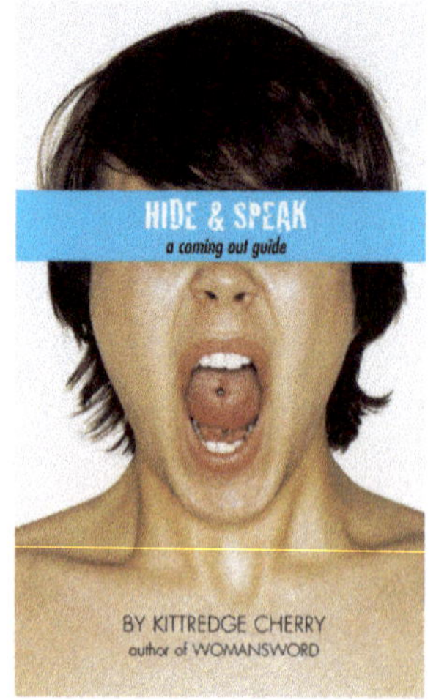

Coming out is easier with this step-by-step guide. Here is practical help with the coming-out process for lesbian, gay, bisexual, and transgender people—and anyone else with a story to tell. Find positive ways to: come out to yourself, create a circle of supporters, deal with family, choose whether to stay "in the closet" at school or work, live proud, free and balanced—no matter what happens. *Hide and Speak* guides readers on a journey that can change their lives.

"Kitt Cherry takes us on a life-changing journey into those hidden places where our secrets lie waiting in the shadows. With examples that inspire and inform, she helps us understand the difference between secrets that kill and secrets that give life. How much suffering I could have avoided for myself and others if only I had read this book before blundering out of my own darkness into the light. This handbook for 'coming out' is not just for sexual minorities but for all people who struggle with secrets and their consequences. And don't skip over the exercises at the end of each chapter. They work!"

—Rev. Dr. Mel White, Founder of Soulforce and author of *Religion Gone Bad: The Hidden Dangers of the Christian Right,*

"A deeply honest, perceptive book. Kittredge Cherry helps us all to understand that the journey into the fullness of humanity is identical with the journey into God. She comes out of her closet and calls her readers to do the same, no matter what their closets might be."

—Bishop John Shelby Spong, Author of *The Sins of Scripture: Exposing the Bible's Texts of Hate in Search of the God of Love*

"In *Hide and Speak*, Kittredge Cherry achieved a wise, witty and wonderful balance, honoring human secrets yet at the same time teaching us why, when, and how to reveal them to others. This is a helpful guidebook, reader-friendly and timelessly relevant for people in all stages and walks of life—but especially for LGBT people who are thinking about opening their closet doors."

—Virginia Ramey Mollenkott, Author of *Omnigender* and *Sensuous Spirituality*

"Coming out is the heroic deed that every gay person has to accomplish. A lifetime of happiness awaits. It helps to do it well. It helps to have a guide. *Hide and Speak* is just that guide. Kitt Cherry gives sensible and wise directions for the lesbian and gay hero journey."

—Toby Johnson, Psychotherapist and author of *The Myth of the Great Secret: An Appreciation of Joseph Campbell*; former editor, *White Crane: A Journal of Gay Men's Spirituality*

www.ingramcontent.com/pod-product-compliance
Lightning Source LLC
LaVergne TN
LVHW060601110826
845154LV00004B/108
9781955821490